SEARCH AND RESCUE
ALASKA

ALSO FROM LYONS PRESS:

Search and Rescue Rocky Mountains

SEARCH
AND
RESCUE
— ### ALASKA —

TRACY SALCEDO

LYONS
PRESS

Guilford, Connecticut

LYONS
PRESS

An imprint of The Rowman & Littlefield Publishing Group, Inc.
4501 Forbes Blvd., Ste. 200
Lanham, MD 20706
www.rowman.com

Distributed by NATIONAL BOOK NETWORK

British Library Cataloguing in Publication Information available

Library of Congress Cataloging-in-Publication Data available

ISBN 978-1-4930-3728-5 (paperback)
ISBN 978-1-4930-3729-2 (e-book)

∞™ The paper used in this publication meets the minimum requirements
of American National Standard for Information Sciences—Permanence
of Paper for Printed Library Materials, ANSI/NISO Z39.48-1992.

CONTENTS

PREFACE

Almost all travel in Alaska is wilderness travel. Venture outside town centers, from Utqiaġvik to Ketchikan, from Nome to Chicken, and you enter the bush. Trails are few, and cross-country miles are endless. Great rivers freeze up and break up, swell with snowmelt and subside into intricate braids, branch through endless expanses of tundra and thickets of black spruce. Mountains rise to stunning heights, with uncounted ridge-lines and glaciers yet to be traversed. Maritime moisture waters a rain

Alaska makes you feel small in a big, beautiful way.
PHOTO: TRACY SALCEDO

forest where salmonberry and devil's club weave an impenetrable under-story beneath a canopy of Sitka spruce, western hemlock, and red and yellow cedar. The wilderness is all encompassing, the beauty so intense it blows open the minds of resident Alaskans and visitors alike, entrancing adventurers and seekers from around the world.

It becomes obvious on arrival that in this vastness, you can easily over-estimate your capacity to undertake any task at hand. Having no trail makes it hard to retrace your steps when you lose the way. A river cold but passable in the morning may be a horrific torrent by afternoon, swollen by snowmelt in a distant range. Crevasses on glaciers shift endlessly, yawning like cats' mouths to swallow you whole. The weather is unforgiving. The bears may eat you. The mosquitoes may eat you as well, or just drive you to dangerous distraction. And there's this thing called the Alaskan mile: Whatever your preconception of distance or height, in Alaska it is longer, and it is higher.

No matter your skill, your level of fitness, your detailed prepara-tions, you can easily be overwhelmed, your endurance tested in unex-pected, uniquely Alaskan ways. You can get hurt. You can get lost. You can disappear.

The good news is someone will come looking for you.

INTRODUCTION: THE DIFFERENCE BETWEEN SAR AND A HAM SANDWICH

Whether the mission is to pluck an injured climber off a mountaintop or to find a snow machiner late for a village basketball game, search and rescue (SAR) in Alaska follows a script. Circumstances invariably require deviation, but the basic structure of most operations is well established and field-tested, with success derived from order, discipline, and experience as much as from bravery, sacrifice, and creativity.

When someone needs rescue, Alaska's tight-knit community of federal, state, local, and volunteer agencies pulls from a deep reservoir of resources and skill sets. Traditional hierarchies built into lead organizations like the National Park Service and Alaska State Troopers are important but become malleable in practice; in the field, teammates shelve their egos and do whatever must be done. The person best suited to the job does the job. And there's plenty of talent to choose from.

THE NUTS AND BOLTS OF ALASKAN SEARCH AND RESCUE

It starts with selection of an incident commander from the oversight agency, who coordinates teams formed under his or her authority: the helicopter or air rescue team, the ground rescue team, the logistics team. If the rescue is on land owned by the federal government—more than 60 percent of the state's 424 million acres are within the boundaries of a national park, wildlife refuge, or monument—the park service assumes the lead and a ranger becomes incident commander. If the SAR occurs elsewhere, state troopers often have jurisdiction.

But ranger and trooper are not alone in the field. As one search-and-rescue veteran observes, "If the military weren't involved, the state would be in trouble." The Alaska Rescue Coordination Center, based at Joint Base Elmendorf-Richardson outside Anchorage, provides coordination for both military and civilian air search and rescue. The US Air Force's parajumpers comprise elite units prepared for search and rescue in any setting, from frozen summit to combat zone. According to Denali National Park and

Preserve ranger Mark Westman, parajumpers "get the Pro Award" for their expertise. His example: In 2011, a guided team of four climbers had just begun a descent of the notorious Autobahn on Denali, known as the most dangerous slope on the commonly climbed West Buttress route, when one of the mountaineers slipped. Because they weren't anchored to fixed lines, the team fell more than a thousand feet before coming to rest. Two of the climbers, including the guide, were killed in the event; the others were badly injured.

Rangers enlisted the help of a military pararescue crew that included paramedic Bobby Schnell. Because the accident occurred after dark, airlifting the critically injured, including a man with a severe head injury who was having difficulty breathing, wasn't possible. So there, on the mountainside at more than seventeen thousand feet, Schnell performed a lifesaving cricothyrotomy to open the patient's airway, using a "pocket knife and a straw." When daylight came, the climber was airlifted to recuperate in the hospital.

"These guys are like ninjas," the ranger says.

The state's volunteer SAR organizations are equally valued. Alaska Mountain Rescue Group (AMRG) harnesses the talents of a variety of rescuers, such as handlers of scent dogs for avalanche rescue and swimmers

Andy Hermansky pilots an A-Star B3e helicopter into the Alaska Range for "typical terrain" short-haul training.
NATIONAL PARK SERVICE. PHOTO: DAN CORN

trained for swift-water rescue. AMRG is also a training resource and a clearinghouse for information, as is the Alaska Search and Rescue Association, which works with Alaska State Troopers to train and manage local SAR teams. These volunteers embody the pervasive ethos of search and rescue in the state: Mention SAR anywhere—in restaurants, roadhouses, grocery stores, outdoor retailers, the living rooms of friends' homes—and someone's involved in search and rescue at some level, or knows someone who is.

Likewise, mention rescue in Alaska and the mountaineering rangers of the national and state parks, especially those based in Denali National Park and Preserve, get a respectful nod. Encompassing more than six million acres in the Alaska Range, Denali is a beacon for visitors possessing all levels of backcountry competence, from clueless tourist to seasoned alpinist, and thus, by default, is a hotspot for rescues of all descriptions. Denali's rangers have not only seen a lot, they've successfully dealt with a lot. And they are willing to lend their experience wherever and whenever needed.

Local knowledge is key to a successful SAR mission, given the vastness of the state and its wildly divergent terrain. What works in Anchorage may not apply in Nome; what's needed at 14,200 feet on Denali might be useless on Kruzof Island near Sitka. Folks may be called in from outside to help with an incident, but the volunteers and professionals who know that specific backcountry intimately—the dips of the valleys, where the rivers collide, how the winds blow—have a profound influence on a mission's success. *There's a cabin on the river bend with a cache. These are the coordinates for the closest landing strip. We can pick up survivors from this ridge if the winds cooperate.*

Cross-pollination between entities is integral, and SAR teams incorporate the appropriate skills and resources for a given emergency. Logistical support, overland support, air support, emergency medical training, and communications translate across every search and every rescue. Good communication is essential. Whether you're short-hauling a climber off an icefall or using a chain attached to your bumper to haul a neighbor out of an icy ditch, you need to clearly understand what is needed, what the dangers are, and what resources are available.

Rigging a rescue in practice on the Valdez Glacier.
NATIONAL PARK SERVICE. PHOTO: MELIS COADY

While teams regularly practice the skills they'll need to work efficiently and safely in the field, one rescuer calls success in SAR "odometer based." In the end, those skills are honed on real missions. The process can't be fast-tracked, which is why search-and-rescue teams embrace the participation of those with long histories. Elders may not be the first choice for the sharp end, but their experience and expertise are invaluable.

Another important component in search and rescue is the confidence that anyone on the team, in the room, or in the tent can find a way to fulfill any role in a SAR, within limits. The mountaineer may not be able to fly the helicopter, and the pilot may not be able to scale the icy headwall, but they can reach into a pool of internal or external resources to summon the needed expertise and explore options. Roles may be clear, but in an emergency, flexibility comes into play. Though technically she may not be qualified, one experienced ranger asserts that, if called upon, even Denali's public information officer could spearhead the logistics of a search-and-rescue operation on the mountain. She knows the right questions to ask.

WHO ARE THESE PEOPLE?

Former Denali mountaineering ranger Daryl Miller sits at his dining room table in Anchorage and thinks for a moment. With a treasury of search-and-rescue expeditions notched on his ice ax, he has much to draw upon when asked about risk and reward on alpine ascents in Alaska's backcountry. Think about a ropes course, Miller offers. The perception of risk is greater on the challenges high off the ground, but more injuries occur on the lower level. Think about a road trip to a peak in a distant locale. The perception of risk is focused on the climb, but an accident is more likely to occur on the highway. "What's the real risk?" he asks.

Miller embodies the thoughtfulness and common sense those who work in Alaskan search and rescue must possess to be successful—and to survive. To the layperson, daring and selflessness are the sexier personality traits of any first responder, from the firefighter to the parajumper. But Miller and his colleagues wouldn't be able to do the work if they weren't smart and methodical as well.

Before launching any mission, the men and women of Alaskan SAR carefully consider pros and cons and measure risk and reward. On Denali, for example, once a request for SAR is received, the incident is evaluated on a number of levels, with rangers, pilots, and volunteers working through a set of principles and practices cultivated over years of experience and pre-planning, as well as through analysis of events in their aftermath.

The first question, and the most fundamental: Is this a rescue or a recovery?

Then there's the weather: If it's a rescue, is it a go or a no-go for a helicopter? Is there visibility for a mile? What is the wind's velocity, direction, maximum gust? The terrain is examined: Can the rescue site be accessed from the ground? What can fall on rescuers from above? Rocks? Ice? What lies below? Crevasses? Cliffs?

Miller displays another trait that's typical of the rescuer, and as refreshing as it is necessary. His friend, mountaineer Pat Rastall, laughingly references the "humble contest." Humility is front and center in any conversation about search and rescue. It's as dominant as a passion for mountaineering, or for flying, or for subsistence living in the Alaskan bush.

Which leads to another theme that crops up again and again in conversation with Miller, other rangers, and rescuers from other agencies. The most effective teams are made up of experts who understand they may not be the best at what they do, and who want nothing more than to surround themselves with other experts who are smarter than they are. That doesn't mean people are afraid to raise the red flag: If something strikes someone as a bad idea, they speak up. Discussion follows. Leadership is important but it's not followed blindly, and the leaders are comfortable with the fact that, yes, they can be questioned . . . or replaced.

Which leads to yet another refreshing theme: It's OK to say no. If, for example, an incident commander discovers the mountaineer in need of rescue is a friend, colleague, or family member, they can pull back. *I am too close*, they can say, knowing their intimacy may compromise their ability to make good decisions. And someone else can step in. No judgment except good judgment.

Mesh measured fearlessness, selflessness, and carefully cultivated skills with practicality, experience, a passion for service, and a love of place, and the true heroism of the men and women of Alaskan SAR comes into focus.

"YOUR EMERGENCY IS NOT OUR EMERGENCY"

Though the theme is search and rescue, every story in this book demonstrates the axiom that, at the most basic level, survival in Alaska's backcountry is an individual's responsibility. Being physically and mentally prepared to endure any contingency—getting lost, injured, tired, hungry, pinned down by weather—is paramount. In Alaska, Mother Nature dishes out the unexpected and extreme in heaping shovelfuls. She's a bit like the old woman who lived in a shoe: She can't take care of all her creatures, so she gives them the basics, and sometimes a whipping, and carries on. What goes for the bear and the moose also goes for the human. You've got to be hardy, intuitive, able to adapt.

"It comes down to you and what you have, what you see, and what you've got," Daryl Miller says simply.

The advent of technology has had a profound impact on expectations for those in search and rescue, challenging the long-standing Alaskan mindset of self-sufficiency. Every ranger and rescuer I spoke with mentioned the yin and yang of technology's role in wilderness travel. It's a pervasive theme throughout the north country wildlands and beyond.

On the one hand, it makes perfect sense that everyone should carry tools that will enhance their experience and keep them safe. Cell and satellite phones; global positioning systems; personal locators (SPOT devices); drugs that prevent or relieve symptoms of acute mountain sickness; high-tech clothing and shelters designed to better withstand Arctic weather; the specialized gear used in rescue, from ropes and harnesses to helicopters stripped of all the essentials so they can operate at high altitudes—they've all become integral to the fabric of outdoor endeavor.

But the people who work in SAR are hyper-aware of the pratfalls newfangled devices pose to Alaskan travelers. A level of comfort is conferred upon the hiker, driver, paddler, or alpinist with technology in hand. That comfort is lost when the batteries die or when the connections are lost. The devices may be lifelines, but they don't take the place of food and fuel, solid and adequate gear, and common sense.

It's also important to keep in mind that, even if you call for it, rescue may not be forthcoming. First you have to make it through triage. I've dubbed it the ham sandwich equation (courtesy of conversations with backcountry rangers in Denali). When a request for aid comes in, rangers must determine whether the "victim" is truly in danger of losing life, a limb, or an eye, or whether she just needs a snack. One fellow memorably called for rescue while climbing Mount Foraker because, as it turned out, he was late for work. You may think you've got an emergency but you'd best be prepared to tough it out, because the rescue ain't coming unless the rescuers agree you're in serious trouble.

Even if rescuers determine real risk exists, the response will be measured. One group of mountaineers on Denali, tired and hungry and unable to move because they'd exhausted their gear, called for help and found themselves in receipt of assistance . . . though not the kind they expected. A helicopter was dispatched, but instead of airlifting the climbers off the slopes, the craft hovered and dropped supplies, forcing them to walk down, longtime mountaineering ranger Roger Robinson explained. The response was prudent, and though the mountaineers may have hoped for more, in the end everyone survived.

And rescuers may opt to safeguard their teams by holding back completely. The last thing an incident commander wants to do is watch a trooper, ranger, or volunteer die on a mission. Miller quietly acknowledges that, as an incident commander, he's "had a say" in the deaths of colleagues, giving permission for one to climb, one to look . . . and they never came back. "That's the worst," he says, looking down at his hands.

The lasting impacts of the ultimate sacrifice resonate through the years in places like Denali. In the briefing room at the ranger station in Talkeetna, ranger Mark Vanderbeek regards the viewer from a plaque on the wall, a rope and carabiners slung over a shoulder. He perished while attempting to help a climber on the High One, as Denali is called, in May 1998. Another plaque memorializes four men who lost their lives when a thunderstorm downed their aircraft en route to base camp on the Kahiltna Glacier. Ranger Cale Shaffer, volunteer rangers Adam Kolff and Brian Reagan, and pilot Don Bowers died in the June 2000 accident. These spirits abide in the room where living rangers counsel aspiring summiters about the challenges they will face as they scale the roof of North America. These climbers, too, might become unreachable, unsaveable.

When search is called off or a rescue becomes a recovery, families bear the brunt of the brutalizing blow. The calamity may be draped in layers of complication: Loved ones may struggle to wrap their grief around both the intricacies and dangers of the recovery that must be abandoned, and also the exotic nature of the endeavor—mountain climbing—that's taken the life of a son or daughter, brother or sister. This "chain of pain" links to friends new and old; to neighbors and coworkers in distant hometowns and boroughs; to the rescuers themselves; even to writers recounting the stories many years later.

"Alaska is a big state with a small community," Miller observes. The chain of pain is long and sturdy, and the lessons are fixed in the links, never to be forgotten.

IN PRAISE OF STRENGTH AND GENEROUS SPIRITS

Contemplating the stories to tell in this book, Denali's Roger Robinson admonished me to write only about rescues, not recoveries. I've mostly honored that request, though even the most heroic tales of successful rescues have sad sides. Search and rescue becomes search and recovery with an exhale. But searchers and rescuers don't discriminate. Their mission is to find those lost in the wild and bring them home.

I, however, had to discriminate in choosing these stories. The focus of this book is search and rescue on land, not on water—and primarily on public lands. Within that scope, I sought to span the breadth of the state both geographically and historically. Like that was a reasonable thing to consider for a subject this big in a state this big. For better or worse I've whittled it down to what I believe are the sharpest needles in the proverbial haystack, which means that, like Alaskan miles to be walked, plenty of Alaskan search-and-rescue stories remain untold.

The focus on public lands also fixes the lens on Denali. Stories from both park and peak are beyond compelling, in my view, so it seems right and fair to dedicate many pages to their retelling.

These stories span the gamut from the legendary delivery of life-saving serum via the Iditarod Trail in 1925 to the remarkable retrieval of a mountaineer from an icy crevasse in 2017; from freeing miners buried in avalanche debris to untangling a knot of neophyte climbers after a terrifying chain-reaction fall down a steep mountain couloir. My hope is that, like me, you'll find reason to rejoice in the strength and generosity of spirit that shines from these tales of search and rescue, and that you'll take comfort in knowing that no matter the distance, no matter the trouble, in Alaska, someone will always come looking for you.

ALASKA
FAR AND WIDE

Their names are sprinkled sparingly on the map: Tanana, Bethel, McGrath, Kake, Chicken, Coldfoot, Bettles, Noatak, Utqiaġvik. Villages with a handful to a few hundred year-round residents are scattered across the tundra of the Interior, tucked in bays on the coastlines from Southeast to the Aleutians to Point Barrow, strung like gemstones along snaking rivers winding through mountains and boreal forests. The names of public lands are scattered as well, because the terrain encompassed by each is prodigious. These Wildernesses are synonymous with romance and adventure: Gates of the Arctic and Glacier Bay; Kenai and Katmai; Chugach and Tongass.

The space between and within is primed for escape, exploration, and the possibility of getting profoundly lost.

Search and rescue in these far-flung locales reaches across time, from the days of frontier exploration to the days of the turbo-charged snow machine. But the focus remains on wildlands, whether in a national park or on private land, either of which can encompass thousands of square miles in Alaska.

A handful of the state's national parks and preserves predate statehood, which Alaska achieved in 1959. But a number were created—and the boundaries of others blasted outward—in 1980, with the passage of the Alaska National Interest Lands Conservation Act (ANILCA). This controversial legislation secured more than a hundred million acres in the public domain, creating new parks and refuges in the process, and protecting those lands from exploitation by oil companies and other corporate interests.

ANILCA was transformative on a number of levels. It touched every aspect of life for most Alaskans. Where and how they could live, hunt, and travel were all circumscribed, for better or worse, by provisions of the legislation. Subsistence hunting, for example, is permitted in the national preserves abutting national parks, but not within the new or expanded boundaries of national parks themselves. In newly designated

The proverbial Alaskan mile: It's just over that rise.
PHOTO: TRACY SALCEDO

or expanded Wildernesses, snow machines are prohibited, along with other motorized tools and conveyances; in these places people get around as they did before the internal combustion engine gained a foothold—on foot or via dogsled.

For a population with an independent streak as fierce as winter wind, ANILCA took some getting used to. The initial reaction of many residents was rebellion: President Jimmy Carter, who signed the act into law, was burned in effigy, and everyone from newspaper editors to politicians railed against what they considered theft of land by the federal government. Over the years the rancor has mellowed; Alaskans have begun to reap the economic benefits of tourism in the parklands, as well as the bounty conferred by protections designed to support game populations and fisheries.

In terms of search and rescue, ANILCA codified what terrain and weather already dictated. People are secluded on the landscape. Roads can't be built in designated Wildernesses; airstrips can't be built there either. On the upside, Alaska's most remote parks see little traffic and thus fewer SARs. On the downside, there's no easy access, and no easy way out.

Some things change, and some things stay the same. Before and after ANILCA, Alaskan settlements remain isolated and faraway, and likewise search-and-rescue operations. Scattered, but epic. The stories gathered here reflect how things have changed over the years, and also shine a spotlight on the arguably more important things that haven't.

Overland for the Seafarers

―――――――

Some of the officers of the wrecked vessels . . . were stunned and
it was some time before they could realize that we were flesh and
blood. They looked to the south to see if there was not a ship in sight
and others wanted to know if we had come up in a balloon.
—LIEUTENANT DAVID JARVIS, LEADER OF THE OVERLAND
RELIEF EXPEDITION, UPON HIS ARRIVAL IN POINT BARROW

Adventure literature from the age of exploration is rich with stories of
ships and crews lost on missions of arctic discovery, which was in full
bloom in the late 1800s and early 1900s. In those days both the North Pole
and South Pole were prizes to be claimed, as were the whales, seals, and
otters that flourished in the fertile, frigid seas at world's extremes. Sometimes these expeditions of discovery and fortune met success, sometimes
explorers and fortune seekers simply vanished.

But that didn't mean no one went looking for the disappeared. Even
in those days, before flight or satellite phones or global positioning systems could pinpoint locations, rescue missions were launched. Rescuers
might find themselves in the same wintry void as the missing but they went
anyway, outfitted as thoroughly as possible for unfathomable conditions
on both land and sea. They came to know, as the native Alaskan knows,
that in an arctic winter waterways become highways. The rivers freeze; the
seas solidify and crumple against the shorelines. You'd think in this season
of stunning cold, Alaskans would stay put someplace safe and warm. But
folks got around, to secure supplies, visit relatives and friends, deliver the

Track chart of the Overland Relief Expedition, 1897–1898.
PHOTO COURTESY OF THE US NAVY

mail, except in the fiercest and coldest storms. Those rivers and shorelines become trails for travelers. Rescue for the seafarer often came overland.

Two stories of ships and crews essentially landlocked in pack ice illustrate the interconnectedness of land and water in Alaska. On one occasion, an expedition determined to reach the North Pole via the Bering Strait endured two long winters adrift in the ice, and became the object of a rescue effort that included a legendary American naturalist and wilderness advocate. Less than a decade later the crews of a fleet of whalers trapped in the pack endured a bitter season of starvation while a remarkable overland expedition plowed to their aid, sails and rudders giving way to sleds pulled by dogs and reindeer.

One rescue was successful, the other failed. And both failed in a way that, given the times, probably never occurred to the white men who lived to tell the stories. The cultural oversights are confounding to the modern sensibility, the focus of the rescuers so fixed on the salvation of their white-skinned kin they were mostly oblivious to the needs of others on the winter ice ... except as cultures to be observed, and resources to be mined.

Determination, fortitude, and an unwillingness to abandon mates while hope remains are the threads that run through the tales, but so does the generosity of Alaskan natives, for even as they coped with the demands of the season they also gave what they could to strangers in need.

THE OVERLAND RELIEF EXPEDITION

In the late nineteenth century, the formation of pack ice above the Arctic Circle was notorious for trapping ships that lingered too late in the season, locking them fast, grinding their hulls, and sometimes crushing them. Timing the formation of the pack and predicting how it would move and how long it would last were life-threatening crapshoots, but also risks whalers were willing to take, given the fortunes they could amass with a successful season's bounty.

In September 1897, a fleet of whaling vessels rolled the dice and lost. Ice that wasn't supposed to form until November trapped eight ships off Nuvuk, or Point Barrow, where Alaska spills into the Arctic Ocean. Two-hundred sixty-five whalemen found themselves stranded, undersupplied, and far from home as the winter closed in. One ship, the *Ocra*, was crushed in the ice, and another ship was so badly disabled she had to be abandoned. When it became clear there wasn't room aboard the remaining vessels for all the survivors, some of the men ventured onshore. Charlie Brower, who operated a whaling station on the point, and Ned McIlhenny, a scion of the McIlhenny Tabasco brand company who was in the tiny settlement collecting specimens for the University of Pennsylvania's Natural History Museum, immediately recognized the whalers were in dire straits, and cobbled together roughshod shelter for dozens of the stranded men. Using surplus wood to create bunks in an abandoned building, and warehousing whatever wildlife and fish stocks they could hunt down and preserve before the season shut them down, Brower and McIlhenny created a ramshackle, mostly winterized sanctuary for the men.

But there wasn't enough room in the bunkhouse for all those stranded on the trapped whaling ships, so those crews stayed aboard. On the *Wanderer*, the *Jeannie*, the *Belvedere*, the *Rosario*, and others, men settled in to wait out the season, and Brower and McIlhenny, along with native Alaskans who lived near the whaling station, prepared to provide what support they could.

It was clear from the outset that there wasn't enough food to support the shipwrecked and landlocked for long. If the whalers were to survive, they'd need to be supplied. And then they'd need to be taken home. Hope for that resupply and rescue lay with one of the whaleships, the *Alexander*, which was able to escape before the ice solidified around her. Commanded by Captain Benjamin Tilton, the *Alexander* ran south to San Francisco to relay news of the emergency. The plight of the whalemen, published widely in the florid, evocative fashion of newspapers in the era, captivated the public. Within a month President William McKinley had signed orders authorizing a rescue mission, and by the end of November the Revenue Cutter Service vessel *Bear*, outfitted for Arctic conditions and captained by Francis Tuttle, a veteran of northern seafaring, was steaming from Seattle to the whaleships' aid.

Given the season, it was certain the *Bear* would be turned around by the pack far south of Point Barrow or risk becoming icebound herself, but the men at Point Barrow couldn't be left to die. Since they couldn't be supplied by sea, Captain Tuttle decided they'd be supplied by land. The plan, simple but audacious, was outlined in advance. Tuttle would deposit a small expedition at the northernmost port he could reach. That team would secure a number of reindeer from herders on the mainland and drive the animals cross-country to Point Barrow, delivering the resources that would save the whalers from starvation. Never mind the distance. Never mind the dead of winter.

By mid-December, the *Bear* reached its northernmost limit, unable to make further headway against Alaska's wintry seas. A three-man team led

The Revenue Cutter Bear *works free of pack ice at Point Barrow.*
PHOTO COURTESY OF THE US NAVY

by Lieutenant David Jarvis of the Revenue Cutter Service (later to become the US Coast Guard) went ashore at the village of Tununak, on the Alaskan mainland in what is now the Yukon Delta National Wildlife Refuge—nearly eight hundred miles from Point Barrow as the raven flies, more than fifteen hundred miles distant on foot, and much farther south than had been hoped. The *Bear* retreated to Dutch Harbor to wait out the long dark season. The Overland Relief Expedition was underway.

Though the mission was daunting, the men tasked with the rescue were mostly prepared for the hardships they'd encounter on the long trek to Point Barrow. Jarvis and ship's surgeon Dr. Samuel Call were veterans of Arctic travel, and in addition to their previous experience in Alaska, Jarvis was able to communicate with the Yupiks and Iñupiats that called northwestern Alaska home. The third member of the relief team, Second Lieutenant Ellsworth Bertholf, was a newcomer to the Far North, but possessed the same tempered fearlessness and sense of duty that motivated Jarvis and Call, as well as a desire for redemption. He'd joined the Revenue Cutter Service after being dismissed from the US Naval Academy with "fellow pranksters" following a hazing incident, and now he had the "chance to become what he always really wanted to be—a true hero."

That said, an expedition across the Alaskan frontier in the dead of winter required a heck of a lot more than being brave, preparing wisely for the core-numbing cold, and possessing the language skills to negotiate with the locals. The expedition disembarked equipped with sleds, dogs, and about fifteen hundred pounds of food, tents, firearms, ammunition, tobacco, and other supplies. In the village of Tununak they were able to bolster their hauling resources with more sleds and dogs. But they'd have to be flexible and inventive to succeed—and to survive.

Foremost among the challenges they'd face: the weather. Gales, white-outs, temperatures spiraling tens of degrees below zero . . . Accounts of the expedition describe these hardships in abundance. But the frigid winter storms could be endured with the right gear when travel was possible, or allowed to pass from the shelter of a tent, an abandoned cabin, or a snow house when travel was impossible. Though they began their adventure without that essential gear, eventually Jarvis, Call, and Bertholf outfitted themselves with deerskin parkas, mukluks, and other layers of animal skin, proven over time by the Yupik and Iñupiat (called Eskimos at the time) to protect life and limb through the long Alaskan winters.

The men plowed forward through mind-boggling conditions, and occa-sionally a blizzard would slow progress to a crawl, or stop it altogether. In mid-January, after holing up in a hut for as long as he felt he could without jeopardizing the mission, Jarvis led Call and his team toward Cape Nome, writing, "In the middle of the day we would see the sun, a red ball through the driving snow, but everything else on a level was a winding, blinding sheet. As we worked along, seeing nothing, buffeted about by the fierce gusts, it seemed as if we would certainly pay dearly for our temerity."

The terrain was also demanding in novel ways. On the first long leg of the journey, from Cape Vancouver to the village of St. Michael on the southern shoreline of Norton Sound, the team got a taste of what journey-ing "overland" in Alaska would actually entail. They were forced to break trail for their huskies, which pulled sleds loaded with gear and supplies behind. Mountains were hard enough for both man and dog to climb, especially with overburdened sleds, but posed their greatest danger on the downhill side, where the sleds gained speed quickly and threatened to overrun the dogs who were supposed to be pulling them. The solution was to unhitch the dog teams, wrap chains around the runners, and jump on board the rocketing sleds, hoping the weight and drag would keep speed in check.

Then there was way-finding. To this day few roads or trails traverse the Alaskan bush. The only way the expedition stood a chance of success was by employing local guides, and these had to be hired from villages along the way. The guides could not only lead the way from Cape Vancouver to Point Barrow, but also could direct Jarvis and his team to the reindeer stations where they'd procure the herds they intended to drive north. Unfortunately the guides sometimes proved unreliable, turning back when they became homesick or forced to abandon the mission when they became ill.

Logistics were demanding as well. Among the hardships the rescuers lamented was the difficulty they had hiring fresh dogs in the native villages they passed through as they moved north. The Alaskans who occupied small settlements—and even larger hamlets on Cape Blossom and Point Hope—didn't have much to spare the expedition, both because of the realities of subsistence living (nature is not a supermarket) and the meagerness of the season. Images captured in settlements during the expedition show clusters of villagers huddled against dwellings in harsh sunlight, and while somber countenances were the photographic fashion of the times, the sober faces don't appear feigned for the camera. Dogs were lifelines, both to neighbors and to the sources of meat native Alaskans relied on. Parting with them, no matter how worthy the cause, was a trial.

Still, the natives gave when they could. Though the scarcity of dogs occasionally threatened the viability of the expedition, the rescuers were able to secure fresh dogs and provisions before any situation became dire.

Finally, there was the unexpected. The want of fresh dogs prompted Jarvis and Call to separate from Bertholf within a week of their arrival on land; the second lieutenant was to secure the huskies and meet the others at Unalakleet, on the edge of Norton Sound. That was, essentially, the last time the three would travel together for the next two months.

Bertholf's journey on an inland route was astounding given his lack of experience, and his performance in the extremes was stellar, if tinged with insanity. After missing the Unalakleet rendezvous, and following written instructions Jarvis left behind when he moved on, Bertholf procured more than a thousand pounds of additional supplies, as well as the guides, dog-sleds, and deer sleds he'd need to transport them to the missionary set-tlement at Cape Blossom, where the three would hook up again. But at one point on the journey, Bertholf found himself alone on a mountainside with a runaway dogsled. He'd been holding his huskies as best he could to maintain a safe distance from the sled ahead of him, which was pulled by reindeer (or dinner, if you're a dog). His weight and that of his two native guides had kept the dogs in check, but when a miscommunication resulted in the guides leaving him alone with the sled, the young lieutenant found himself hurtling up a mountainside, his dogs out of control and in hot pur-suit of reindeer meat.

Bertholf did everything he knew to slow or stop the huskies, who were gaining on the deer. When nothing worked, he slipped down the centerline of the dog team and between the runners of the sled, then used his body weight to capsize it. Once the runners were in the air and the load was grinding through the snow, the dogs slowed to a halt. Tipping the sled was an act of both desperation and derring-do: Bertholf understood that if he couldn't stop the dog team before it caught the reindeer team, all could be lost. The Overland Relief Expedition had come too far to let that happen.

Meantime, Jarvis and Call were wrestling with their own sleds, their own dogs, their own guides, and their own mixed luck. They battled frost-bite and weather delays, natives unwilling or unable to supply fresh dogs, and a steep learning curve when they incorporated sleds pulled by deer into their repertoire. They also had an extraordinary encounter in a snow-storm as they headed north from St. Michael toward Unalakleet. At first Jarvis mistook the sight for a "mirage": A native woman appeared out of the whiteout—someone Jarvis was acquainted with—and she revealed that, with her husband, she was guiding a "white man" south to the port of call. The man was whaler George Tilton of the *Belvedere*, who'd been dispatched by the captains of the trapped ships to seek aid. The situation Tilton relayed was desperate: The captains in Point Barrow estimated they had enough food to sustain the whalers on scant rations until July. They hoped Tilton would reach St. Michael, find transport south, and then lead help back to Point Barrow before the rations ran out.

The three men who spearheaded the Overland Relief Expedition were Commanding Lieutenant David Jarvis (right), Second Lieutenant Ellsworth Bertholf (left), and ship's surgeon Samuel Call (center).
PHOTO COURTESY OF THE US NAVY

While weather and logistics posed unknowns, the reindeer did not. The deer had been imported to Alaska as part of a broader humanitarian rescue mission just years before. The territory's First Peoples had relied on native caribou and fish stocks for centuries prior to colonization, but those stocks had been depleted over the preceding decades by hunters from Russia, America, and Europe, resulting in starvation and the proliferation of disease among the indigenous tribes. American officials began transporting reindeer from Siberia starting in the late 1800s, hoping to alleviate the crisis. The *Bear* was one of the cutters employed on this mission of mercy, and Lieutenant Jarvis had been on the *Bear* for the first of those deliveries. This was a plus: Jarvis not only knew where to find the reindeer stations, but he knew the herders. It took some doing, and promises of reciprocity and reimbursement, but Jarvis was able to convince Charlie Artisarlook, an indigenous reindeer herder, and Tom Lopp, a missionary with a reindeer station on Cape Prince of Wales, to sacrifice a portion of their livelihoods for the benefit of the stranded whalemen. Artisarlook helped drive more than 130 deer north to Lopp's reindeer station, and then Lopp agreed to leave home and family to drive a combined herd—more than 400 animals—north to Point Barrow.

Meanwhile, on the northernmost coastline, the stranded whalemen were falling short of the self-preservation ideal. Filthy, starving, despondent, unmotivated, insubordinate, lazy; the men on the isolated point had succumbed, in some fashion or other, to the Alaskan winter scourge of cabin fever. When Jarvis and his colleagues finally reached Point Barrow after their hundred-day odyssey, they found the seamen in deplorable condition. There'd be no respite for the rescuers: Their first order of business was to make sure the men of the fleet, both in the bunkhouse and on the icebound ships, were fed, cleaned up, and put to work. They'd delivered more than 380 reindeer, so food was no longer an issue, and the meat also addressed one of the many health concerns Dr. Call had to address: Scurvy, caused by malnutrition (specifically a lack of vitamin C), afflicted many of the whalers, and the resources were now on hand to halt progression of the disease.

With the arrival of Jarvis, Call, Lopp, and the reindeer herd, the immediate emergency was resolved. But the rescue wouldn't be complete until the *Bear* returned to pick everyone up and transport them back to the Lower 48, which would only be possible once the midnight sun returned in summer and the sea ice melted. To enhance survival in the long months ahead, Jarvis secured additional quarters for the whalers so they weren't crammed in squalid conditions. The officers knew idle bodies led to idle minds, or worse, so as the days grew longer they devised a number of unexpected and ingenious activities for the men—baseball games, duck-hunting parties, ten-mile slogs to retrieve the ducks shot by the hunters—which proved effective motivators and improved the overall well-being of everyone stuck in Point Barrow.

The final component of the rescue was underway by mid-June, when the *Bear* departed Dutch Harbor and steamed north as quickly as she could. She picked up troublesome news along the way—the men at the Point would be out of food by August 1. Another one of the whaling ships, the *Rosario*, had been destroyed in early July, undermined by shifting floes driven against her hull in a huge storm, and her crew was now ashore as well. The *Bear* steamed into view with only a few days to spare, on July 28, having stopped at the *Belvedere* to drop supplies to the men who'd overwintered on board.

Jarvis, Tuttle, Call, Bertholf, and the whalers would face one more challenge before all was said and done. On August 1, with everyone aboard and the safety of Seattle the next stop, ice closed in around the *Bear*. For two weeks the men waited, hoping for clear water and a way forward. A shift in the wind and a parting of the ice finally allowed the vessel to escape. The *Bear*, with all aboard, steamed toward home.

She arrived in Seattle in mid-September, to a reception that writer Martin Sandler describes as markedly subdued, considering the ballyhoo that accompanied the rescue at its outset: "The whalemen had been saved. It was an incredible story, but amazingly, there were no headlines." The Spanish-American War was underway, and news of heroic exploits in the Far North had been overshadowed by news of the heroics by America's future president, Theodore Roosevelt, in the Philippines.

But the bravery, toughness, and persistence of Jarvis, Call, and Bertholf, along with others who aided in the remarkable rescue, did not go unrewarded. The men of the Revenue Cutter Service received Congressional Gold Medals, and both Jarvis and Bertholf went on to command the *Bear*, which would continue her service in Arctic waters and become one of the most celebrated cutters in the US Coast Guard. Bertholf later was appointed to the highest post in the Coast Guard née Revenue Cutter Service, appointed captain-commandant in 1911.

The story of the Overland Relief Expedition competes with any in the literature of polar exploration. They may have accomplished incredible things, but no other Arctic adventurers drove a herd of reindeer successfully across fifteen hundred miles of frozen tundra in the dead of winter—not to claim a prize of some sort, but to rescue their fellow men. The

Members of the Overland Relief Expedition pose with a sled at Point Barrow.
Photo courtesy of the US Navy

exploits of the expedition are one of a kind, and set a high bar for those participating in Alaskan search and rescue into modern times.

THE SEARCH FOR THE *JEANNETTE*

When John Muir journeyed to Alaska in 1881, his primary focus was on the rocks. He was a naturalist, after all. The champion of California's Sierra Nevada and future father of the National Park Service joined the crew of the steamship *Thomas Corwin*, bound for the Last Frontier, hoping to gather evidence to back his hypothesis that the massive granite monoliths of his beloved Yosemite Valley were sculpted by glaciers—not a popular view in those days. And the northern territory was full of glaciers and monoliths.

But the mission of the *Corwin* was not focused solely on geologic inquiry. She had standard tasks to carry out over the short summer—enforcing American laws governing fishing and the fur trade; delivering mail; restricting the trafficking of illicit substances like rum and whiskey. She was also charged with a search and rescue. Muir, by default, became one of the hopeful rescuers.

Two years before, in the summer of 1879, the *Jeannette*, a refurbished steamer commanded by George De Long and outfitted for navigation in icebound Arctic seas, had departed the port of San Francisco on a quest of discovery. She had not returned. A pair of whaling vessels sailed into the same waters at the same time, and their fates were also unknown. The *Corwin* was tasked with determining the fate of the *Jeannette* and the whalers, if possible, and with rescuing their crews, if necessary.

The *Jeannette* had ventured into the Arctic on the assumption that a warm Pacific current penetrated what nineteenth-century experts postulated was open sea surrounding the North Pole. Discovery of a polar route—and perhaps the fabled Northwest Passage—was a much sought-after prize for explorers, on a par with reaching the South Pole and exploring the dark heart of Africa.

But neither the warm current nor the polar sea existed as imagined. The *Jeannette* became icebound when winter descended, which wasn't unexpected. But she remained locked in the floes far longer than anticipated. In those long, dark months, sailors became trekkers. The way to anywhere—settlements, food sources, even salvation—was overland and frozen. Sled dogs were better suited to travel than sails.

Though the ship and her crew charted hundreds of miles of unexplored territory on her long drift in the sea ice, De Long's mission was ultimately thwarted by the unrelenting cold and dwindling supplies. He attempted to head south, toward home, but the ice held fast, and eventually the *Jeannette* was crushed by the pack in the East Siberian Sea. At the same time the *Corwin* was en route to their rescue, the *Jeannette*'s crew was making a desperate dash for the Siberian mainland over shifting ice. Only a handful of men survived the long journey by small boat and on foot, eventually making their way through the delta of the Lena River to remote Russian settlements, where they were able to arrange passage home. De Long was not among them; he and a handful of his men perished on the Russian mainland as autumn bled into winter.

But Muir, the *Corwin*'s captain Calvin Hooper, and the rest of the ship's crew had no idea of the fate of the doomed *Jeannette* as they sailed northward. Hope remained in those summer months, and even if they could not bring back the men themselves, they hoped to bring back word of their fate. At ports along the long Alaskan coastline, teams from the steamer ventured onshore, hoping the inhabitants of these far-flung outposts would have a story to tell, or that someone from the *Jeannette* herself had left sign of her passage.

Given all there was to see and study on the Alaskan journey, Muir the naturalist was enchanted and inspired. His observations are collected in *The Cruise of the* Corwin, in which he describes Arctic landscapes and glaciation; flora and fauna; ports of call from Unalaska to Herald Island. He also wrote about the native peoples who called those seaside villages home, describing how the *Corwin* came to anchor "near an Eskimo village at the northwest end of St. Lawrence Island. It was blowing and snowing at the time, and the poor storm-beaten row of huts seemed inexpressibly dreary through the drift. Nevertheless, out of them came a crowd of jolly, well-fed people, dragging their skin canoes . . . soon they were alongside the steamer, offering ivory, furs, sealskin books, etc., for tobacco and ammunition."

In another entry, however, Muir bore witness to the aftermath of a singular, heartbreaking human struggle on St. Lawrence. Earthquake, avalanche, sea wave, wildfire ... even survivors of these disasters might have a difficult time wrapping their heads around what Muir and his crewmates encountered on another stretch of those secluded shores. Though the island's indigenous residents had a deep understanding of the cycles of the Arctic and the subsistence resources it offered, entire communities were decimated by the horrific pairing of disease and starvation that had its genesis in colonialism. The ravages of the killing combination were tapering at the turn of the twentieth century; by then, in the Lower 48, the American Indian Wars had exacted their murderous toll, and culture and genetics had selected the strongest and smartest of those who remained for survival. But in the planet's most distant locales, like the islands of the Bering and Chukchi Seas, isolated from explorers from the Old World and the New, the tragedy was still unfolding.

The *Corwin* dropped anchor near the mouth of Metchigme Bay. There Muir and his colleagues "met a few Eskimos who, though less demonstrative, seemed quite as glad to see us as those on the northwest end of the island. The village as we examined it through our glasses, seemed so still and desolate, we began to fear that ... not a soul was left alive in it, until here and there a native was discovered on the brow of the hill where the summer houses are." Muir and others from the ship were led by survivors to the inhabited houses. Asking where the owners of the other houses were, the natives replied, "All mucky"—all dead.

"We then inquired where the dead people were," Muir wrote. "They pointed back of the houses and led us to eight corpses lying on the rocky ground. They smiled at the ghastly spectacle of the grinning skulls and bleached bones appearing through the brown, shrunken skin."

The *Corwin* didn't rescue the survivors of the stricken villages. The natives, though found, were as lost as the crew of the *Jeannette*, isolated by both culture and location. The white men were on a mission, so the islanders were left behind. Perhaps they had no expectation of rescue. Muir's narrative doesn't reflect on their future, only on their present. The naturalist makes no mention of overt despair. He doesn't record whether the survivors begged to board the *Corwin*. Maybe they were shell-shocked; maybe they hadn't had time to process the depth of their loss and need. Maybe, even though their world was shattered, they knew they could survive. Or maybe they were ready to die.

The *Corwin* continued northward in what was left of that summer, exploring shorelines on the Alaskan and Siberian mainlands and on American and Russian islands as weather and pack ice allowed. The crew was able to confirm the loss of the two whaling ships, but the disposition of the *Jeannette* remained unknown. They navigated again toward Wrangell Land (now called Wrangel Island, a large landmass in Russian waters off the Siberian coastline). Scouting a way to make landfall, hoping to be able to continue their search, Muir and the crew "gazed at the long stretch of wilderness which spread invitingly before us, and which we were so eager to explore—the rounded, glaciated bosses and foothills, the mountains, with their ice-sculptured features of hollows and ridges and long withdrawing valleys, which in former visits we had sketched, and scanned so attentively through field-glasses, and which now began to wear a familiar look."

But Muir was not destined to set foot on the island this time around. "In view of the condition of the ship, and the ice, and the weather, the risk attending further efforts this year to search the shores of Wrangell Land should not be incurred, more especially since the position and drift of the ice held out but little promise of allowing another landing to be made," he wrote. Come the first of September, with winter howling southward, Captain Hooper abandoned the search for the *Jeannette* and turned his steamer toward home.

The *Corwin* returned to the warmer waters of San Francisco Bay without having rescued anyone; not a stricken Arctic native or a lost Arctic explorer. Her quest, however, offers insights into themes that permeate Alaskan search and rescue into modern times. One is the shape-shifting quality of earth and water: how frozen sea ice becomes solid ground and provides a connection between villages and people. Another is the concept of self-rescue. In the Arctic, your ability to save yourself is your one certainty; a successful search and rescue is not. The crew of the *Jeannette* knew this, and did their best to find a way over land and sea to salvation. For the natives of St. Lawrence Island, salvation was something they couldn't walk to; they had to generate it for themselves.

And John Muir? The consummate observer and survivor, a man who stood on a Yosemite cliff and was pounded by a waterfall, who forayed into avalanches of rock ripped from cliff sides by earthquakes, who climbed a tree in a windstorm to decipher its motion—no matter his wilderness skills and his intellect, he too, in this instance, was powerless to bring home the lost.

Avalanche on the Chilkoot Trail

―――――

To-night many of them are sleeping beneath thousands of tons of snow and ice.
―FROM AN ACCOUNT OF THE PALM SUNDAY AVALANCHE
PUBLISHED IN A MISSOURI NEWSPAPER

In 1898 the men who moil for gold descended on Canada's Yukon Territory, where nuggets of the precious metal had been discovered in placer deposits on the Klondike River. As had been the case in California's Sierra Nevada fifty years earlier, the rush began with a proverbial flash in the pan, was followed by a flood of hopeful but hopelessly ill-prepared humanity, and ended with a mass exodus of disappointed souls.

The mentality of a stampeder hardly gels with that of someone dedicated to search and rescue. When you think about the people involved in SAR, selfless individuals with astonishing skill sets come to mind, devoted to service and possessing hearts of gold, not looking for the stuff. Those seeking pockets full of gold were a single-minded, self-centered population, and while some who set out for the Klondike might have been driven by a desire to provide for family, looking out for number one was a way of life on the long trek to Dawson City. Even friends and partners, no matter how solid the bond before the rush, eventually became competitors; after all, not every claim pierced the mother lode. Relationships splintered as spectacularly as river ice during breakup, leaving lonely, desperate people to fend for themselves in the unforgiving woods and squalid boomtowns along the trail.

The spirit of SAR was rare even as the competition dwindled and bailed out. Those who died en route to the goldfields may have been comforted

Chilkoot Pass. 1897

Prospectors make the long slog up the Chilkoot Pass in 1897.
KLONDIKE GOLD RUSH NHP MUSEUM COLLECTION, NATIONAL PARK SERVICE

by a comrade or two, but just as likely not. Others, overwhelmed by the rigors of the journey, let down by the self-serving characters of their human companions, and with empty wallets, headed home as soon as they could. Save the barkeeps and dancehall girls who made fortunes collecting the dust prospectors scratched from their claims, no one missed them, offered them solace, or helped them on their way.

The spirit of SAR in the Klondike rush? Try Stingy and Ruthless.

Even as stories of psychological and physical hardship leaked out of the distant north, thousands of hopefuls were not dissuaded. Gold fever was an incurable addiction, and it was catching. Men and women flooded to the Yukon, no matter the temperature, the terrain, or the trouble.

In one spectacular instance, however, stampeders demonstrated that even within their maverick ranks, kindness and sacrifice could prevail. On one snowy spring day the trail to fortune became a trail of terror and heartbreak, and instead of plowing forward relentlessly in search of riches, men and women paused to plow through avalanche debris in search of buried comrades.

Miners followed several year-round routes to reach Dawson City, a raw, colorful boomtown that sprang up along the banks of the Yukon River near its confluence with the Klondike. Two of the most famous, or infamous, trails were Alaska born. The trail over White Pass began in Skagway, another boomtown that erupted like a zit at the head of the Lynn Canal, in the northernmost reaches of the Inside Passage. By all accounts, the White Pass Trail was a nightmare of the first degree. It was mountainous, blasted by blizzards at any time of year, plagued by crooks in the employ of the dastardly Soapy Smith, and eventually paved in the carcasses of horses abandoned by miners along the way.

Another overnight boomtown sensation, Dyea, the mouth of the Taiya River, served as the starting point for the trail over Chilkoot Pass. The short-lived town was a one-shop outpost before the Klondike strike, exploded like a handful of confetti when the stampeders arrived, and thrived for little more than a year before fading away. The Chilkoot Trail, like the trail over White Pass, was wickedly steep, plagued by storm, and frequented by con artists, but according to one historian it had a major advantage over the neighboring slog: It was not a linear equine graveyard.

The Chilkoot had long been used by local Tlingit bands as a year-round trade route, linking the people of coastal First Nations to those in Alaska's Interior. But that in no way qualified it as a major thoroughfare. The newly arrived prospector, or cheechako, had to move his or her entire outfit—a literal ton of goods—up a river, through a gorge, and then up to the summit of a mountain range that rose nearly four thousand feet straight from the sea, with great glaciers strung like garlands across the summits.

The miners had no choice about the ton of goods: Canada's Royal Mounted Police quickly tired of rescuing stranded miners on their side of the border and set up a way station at Chilkoot Pass where they enforced the onerous requirement. The outfit had to include everything a person would need to survive the long passage to the goldfields and to support a reasonable existence in Dawson City: tens of pounds of flour, oatmeal, and sugar; cured meats and preserved fruit; soap, matches, hammers, nails, saws, and other tools; boots, oilskins, extra socks, mittens; a Yukon sled; and mosquito netting, of course. The prospectors brought goodies along as well. As historian Pierre Berton puts it in *The Klondike Fever*, "Whisky and silk, steamboats and pianos, live chickens and stuffed turkeys, timber and glassware, bacon and beans, all went over on men's backs."

As you might imagine, moving an outfit from town to pass required stampeders to make multiple trips. It could take as long as three months to transport load after load over the summit. Stops along the way allowed the trekkers to catch their breath and lose their money. Miners trudged past Finnegan's Point to Canyon City, a kind of base camp at riverside near the mouth of the gorge, where a pair of tramway operations built their power-houses and set about hoisting gear to the pass for a fee. It was all uphill from Canyon City to Pleasant Camp, and then to Sheep Camp, another major waypoint just below tree line. In these inhospitable locations prospectors built teardown towns, boxes stacked and tents erected only to be uprooted when it was time to move on, then quickly replaced by the tents and boxes of the next wave of the Klondike-bound.

Miners climb the Golden Stairs on the Chilkoot Trail.
CANDY WAUGAMAN'S COLLECTION, NATIONAL PARK SERVICE

Above Sheep Camp, without cover of trees, the exposure increased, and glaciers dripped down the steep mountainsides. Brief respite was available at Stone House, where an overhanging rock provided some shelter. The last stop was the Scales, a sprawling camp in the bowl below the pass, called "one of the most wretched spots on the trail." Here any pack animals who'd survived were abandoned, since no matter the season they couldn't manage the last brutal stretch of the ascent. During the summer it was thirty-five degrees of exposed talus and boulders. During the long winter more than a thousand steps—the Golden Stairs—were chipped into the icy slope. The black-and-white photographs of the snowbound pitch are iconic: A line of stampeders in single file on the white face of the mountain, with no visible separation between, marching up to a notch in the jagged ridgeline.

After the Mounties confirmed possession of the requisite supplies at the Canadian border, a prospector could move on, downhill to Crater Lake, Happy Camp, Lake Lindeman, and finally Bennett Lake, where he could build a boat and set sail for Dawson City. This may have been a relief to the footsore: By one estimate, some gold seekers logged a thousand miles just to get their goods to the Canadian checkpoint. But there were still hundreds of miles to go, and not a one of them was easy.

Seasoned travelers in the coastal mountains—including the Tlingit, who had called Southeast Alaska home for centuries—knew the slopes were primed for disaster when the snow fell long and thick. Spring is notorious for avalanche along the Chilkoot Trail into modern times. Storms deposit heavy, wet loads on slopes approaching the angle of repose, between thirty and forty-five degrees, where they settle in layers that sometimes compact and stabilize, and sometimes don't. When warmed by sun, triggered by rockfall, or set off by the footfalls of men, slabs like great, slick, white plates fracture free and career down mountainsides, gathering volume and velocity as they descend. They scour the slopes of everything in their paths—trees, shrubs, rocks, and people.

But the threat posed by heavy deposits in the winter of 1897–1898 wasn't foremost in the mind of the argonaut hauling his lumber, lard, and hardware toward the promised land. He was in for a quick and brutal lesson in a mountaineering reality: avalanche.

In February and March 1898 incessant storms deposited heavy snowfall on the steep slopes surrounding the Chilkoot Trail. A warm wind then blew through, creating a weak layer in the snowpack. This was followed by more heavy snowfall. According to one historical account, both native Alaskans and settlers who'd been in the territory for a while refused to head up the trail in those early days of April. "There was so much snow I did not see how it could cling to the sides of the canyon," one prospector told the *San Francisco Call*. "Great fields and mountains of it were piled upon the top of the canyon on both sides." Anyone with snow sense, even a California cheechako, knew conditions were sketchy.

And sure enough, on Palm Sunday, April 3, 1898, snowfields surrounding the trail, clotted with men and beasts hoping to take advantage of a break in the storm, began to fracture and collapse.

Five avalanches thundered down onto the burdened trekkers that hellish day. The first occurred early that morning, and buried twenty stampeders near the Scales. A miner who'd witnessed the event, described by

Berton as "a bent old man, groaning and waving his arms," raised the alarm, and these victims were rescued by fellow prospectors.

Though not technically search and rescue, warnings traveled along the trail, no doubt saving a number of lives. Men and women at the Scales who were transporting goods or working the tramways began to descend toward the safety of Sheep Camp. Their retreat was accompanied by the sinister cracks and booms of avalanche releases, which offer the observer, or victim, a moment to look up, freak out, and do their best to get out of the way.

The second slide occurred later that morning, and buried another three fortune seekers. Again, all three were rescued. But snow continued to dump from the heavens, and the mountains continued to dump their loads. More than two hundred prospectors and others, including workers employed by the Chilkoot Railroad and Transport Company, were doing their best to skedaddle, but were confounded by whiteout conditions as the weather worsened. They hitched themselves to a rope and followed the leader down toward safety.

The next slide was the first killer. It buried a camp below Squaw Hill, crushing three prospectors in their tents. It also tumbled Marc Hanna, an ox, but somehow the animal was able to create an envelope in the debris—a cave of snow—and survived the ordeal. Uncovered and unharmed, the ox was employed in the removal of avalanche victims to burial in Dyea, according to a park service history.

A party of workers for the Chilkoot tramway company were the next victims, caught in a slide on a side trail that passed through a steep ravine. Just why the men were in that ravine, and which way they were traveling, is a matter of conjecture. But in the whiteout conditions the victims may have wandered off-route, and everyone caught in that flow perished.

The fifth slide was the most devastating. About two hundred people remained strung out on the rope as they descended from the Scales, following the path broken by the tramway workers. They entered what was called the "drow-a-low" ravine, off-route and in the danger zone, near midday. And the snowpack broke.

This photo was taken near the site of the deadly avalanche by a film crew in 1922.
GEORGE AND EDNA RAPUZZI COLLECTION, RASMUSON FOUNDATION, KLONDIKE GOLD
RUSH NATIONAL HISTORICAL PARK, PRINT INVENTORY # 000583

The slide overtook the people at the front of the line, and swept them away. In his account of the disaster, writer Berton quotes one survivor, J. A. Rines, who described the start of the slide: "All of sudden I heard a loud report and instantly began to feel myself moving swiftly down the hill and, looking round, saw many others suddenly fall down, some with their feet in the air, their heads buried out of sight in the snow." Victims were buried twenty to fifty feet deep along 150 feet of the side trail, their bodies encased in a debris field that covered ten acres.

As modern skiers and alpinists along the Pacific Coast of North America well know, maritime snow sets up instantly, becoming cementlike. In the tumble of an avalanche, the lucky may find themselves trapped in an air pocket, with hope that someone will dig them out before they suffocate or succumb to hypothermia. Others may find themselves mercifully close to the surface, an arm or a leg or a piece of clothing or equipment hinting at where they came to rest, increasing the odds for a swift and successful rescue. Still others may be trapped loosely enough to dig themselves out. But for those buried deeply in the Chilkoot avalanche, the chances of survival were slim, even with hundreds of rescuers on the scene.

One of those at the back of the ill-fated line, a survivor, rushed down to Sheep Camp with the terrible news. It couldn't have been unexpected: The roar of the massive slide had been heard in the camp. The call to action for the search-and-rescue operation was a volley of gunfire. The scale of the effort was immense: More than a thousand formerly self-absorbed stampeders became first responders and rushed to the scene, which Berton describes as a "weird and terrible one." Survivors buried in the debris could be heard talking below, and air holes punctured the surface, hinting at where the living were entombed.

The Palm Sunday event predated avalanche transceivers and telescoping probe poles by decades, so rescuers made do with the equipment in their tons of goods. They dug "parallel trenches" to reach those buried, some of whom survived for three hours encased in the debris before they were freed. Picks and shovels and grit were employed without a second thought; teamwork was born of necessity and shared horror. "In a rare display of unanimity and selflessness, the stampeders abandoned their collective trek in order to rescue and locate the snow slide victims," a park service history explains. "A tent in Sheep Camp was donated for use as a morgue, and the local Citizens' Committee, appointed at a miners' meeting, officially presided over the processing of the bodies for shipment and burial."

"From Sheep Camp to the summit there [were] hundreds of tents," a survivor from Missouri wrote in a letter published in the *Cape Girardeau Democrat*. "All day 2,000 or 3,000 men have been hard at work with shovels taking out the bodies of dead comrades. It is estimated that there are 200 or 300 men and women beneath this mighty weight of snow and ice."

And some of the rescues were "strange," according to Berton's account. One woman was "hauled from the snow where she had been buried head-down, hysterical but living." Another man, a restaurateur named Joppe, was presumed dead when he was pulled from the debris. His "sweetheart" draped herself over his body, mourning and praying and "breathing warm air into his lungs.... For three hours she continued in this manner while those around tried to drag her away. Then, to the stupefaction of all, Joppe suddenly opened his eyes and spoke her name, and it was as if a dead man had miraculously come alive again."

Historians disagree on just how many stampeders were dug out of the main slide alive. The National Park Service, which runs the Klondike Gold Rush National Historical Park, puts the number at ten—and notes that several of those died subsequently of "exposure." But the park service also cites reports that as many as a hundred survivors were pulled from the debris, including a story from the *Dyea Press* asserting fifty people "were pulled from the snow pack because they held onto the communal rope."

There's also confusion about how many gold seekers died in the slide. The various lists include the names of forty to seventy victims, but the names aren't the same and the veracity of the lists isn't solid. One comes from the "headboards" in the Dyea Slide Cemetery, but the park service believes this is incomplete because some of the dead were shipped home for burial and weren't interred in the graveyard at the base of the Chilkoot Trail.

It would be good to believe the spirit of selflessness that characterized the aftermath of the slide was sustained and ubiquitous, but that wasn't the case. Skagway's scoundrel Soapy Smith, devious even in the face of tragedy, reportedly had himself appointed coroner after the slide and proceeded to "[strip] the bodies of cash, jewelry and other valuables." And newspaper accounts of the slide are appended, even in the same story, with descriptions of those who continued into the Klondike, undeterred by the monumental tragedy.

These days, forecasters can predict when avalanche danger is severe, issue warnings, and thus save lives. These days, most backcountry travelers in winter, whether on skis, snowshoes, dogsleds, or snow machines, carry the expertise and equipment to help them determine if the slope they are about to cross is likely to give way, and also the beacons, probes, and shovels they'll need to search for and rescue a companion caught in a slide. In modern Alaska a reprise of the Chilkoot tragedy is a distant possibility. But a reprise of the communal rescue, no matter the circumstance, has become tradition.

Iditarod

———

Y ou could argue no search was involved in the Great Serum Run to save the children of Nome from diphtheria. The place was on the map. But getting to the stricken town, via dogsled in the dead of winter, on a shape-shifting "trail" defined and redefined by storm and wind, all the while safeguarding a precious cargo of life-saving medicine, required way-finding skills, ingenuity, teamwork, and a statewide commitment to the greater good that resonates into modern times.

In 1925 Nome was more than a decade past its heyday as a boomtown. Starting in 1899 prospectors who'd struck out in Canada's Klondike—but hadn't been broken by Alaskan hardships or cured of their gold fever— turned their sights westward, to the coastline of the Bering Sea. A trio of prospectors known as the Lucky Swedes had discovered a placer lode on Anvil Creek, which flowed into the sea near Cape Nome. The mining was reportedly relatively straightforward and, of course, wildly productive: With the right tools and a whole lot of elbow grease, the gold could be sifted from the alluvial sands of rivers and streams and, it was later discovered, from the beaches themselves.

The stampede was on. Thousands of tents took root along waterways and beaches on the coastline of Norton Sound surrounding the mouth of the Snake River. That sprawling tent city quickly became a permanent settlement with all the accouterments of a frontier mining town, including a generous supply of saloons and brothels.

Many of Nome's gold seekers arrived on board ships via the Bering Sea in the summer season. Though arguably easier than the brutal trails leading into the Klondike, angry seas and crowded conditions rendered the journey a trial. When the sea was frozen—which was the bulk of the year—Nome's residents needed another way to get in and out of town, as well as a lifeline to family and friends on the Outside, access to supplies from other parts of the territory, and a link to neighboring mining towns. An overland mail-and-freight route was established: the Iditarod Trail, linking Nome to Seward on the Kenai Peninsula, a thousand miles distant. The trail incorporated dogsled and snowshoe routes used for generations by Alaska's First Peoples and, like other mail routes throughout the great state, generally traced great rivers, as did the trails linking coastal settlements like Anchorage and Seward to Fairbanks, and then Fairbanks to the hinterlands—Circle and Fort Yukon, Tanana and Kantishna, Kotzebue and Nome. The Iditarod followed two of Interior Alaska's largest rivers, the Tanana and the Yukon, before branching north toward Norton Sound.

The Iditarod Trail in winter, like other mail routes in the territory, was no cakewalk. The carriers were mushers, men of remarkable physical and mental strength, many former gold miners tempered by wind, weather, and hard labor. They thrived on the challenge of the bush and demonstrated superhuman abilities to withstand the extremes. The mettle of such Alaskan luminaries as Harry Karstens was honed on mail trails: Karstens's storied career as a musher and carrier earned him history-making invitations to join the team that would claim the first ascent of Denali, to join Charles Sheldon on a yearlong study of wildlife credited with fostering creation of Mount McKinley National Park (now Denali National Park and Preserve), and to serve as that park's first superintendent.

The mushers are, and remain, fierce caretakers of their dogs, nurturing generations of huskies strong, smart, and ideal for the task. Use of sled dogs in the Arctic has a long tradition among native Alaskans in the Interior, along the Bering Sea coast, and on the North Slope, so the animals, like the people, have adapted to the environment, both physically and by developing an innate sense of how the land, water, and weather work. Though the physical characteristics of Alaska huskies are divergent—those in Denali park's kennel sport any mash-up of markings in any color—they've been bred for the stamina, temperament, and instinct that make them premier sled dogs. Siberian huskies and malamutes are popular sled-dog breeds as

Denali National Park and Preserve is the only national park that breeds sled dogs, which are used to patrol the wilderness where machines are not allowed.
DENALI NATIONAL PARK AND PRESERVE

well. The snow machine has become the vehicle of choice for travel across snowy tundra and frozen rivers in the bush, but dogsleds remain a vital resource in the state's millions of acres of designated Wilderness, where mechanized vehicles are forbidden. And huskies have another superior feature touted by advocates: Their carburetors don't freeze up.

It was only natural, then, that in those dark winter days, mushers and dogs would emerge as the best hope for Nome's salvation.

By the time children began to fall ill with diphtheria in December 1924, Nome's boom had gone bust and fewer than fifteen hundred people—white settlers and Iñupiats working the goldfields and focused on subsistence living—called the town home. Its hospital, which served surrounding settlements as well, was staffed by a single doctor and a small team of nurses. Initial signs of the outbreak raised suspicions but were easily overlooked—early symptoms of diphtheria mimic those of other viral or bacterial infections such as tonsillitis: a bad sore throat, fever, swollen glands. But a host of distinctive and deadly effects appear as the disease progresses. The stories are gruesome and terrifying, of gray lesions forming in the mouth, then the esophagus, then the lungs, slowly suffocating the victims. For babes and young children, diphtheria becomes quickly fatal.

The bacteria that causes the disease is also highly contagious; it can be spread with a cough, or deposited on doorknobs or schoolhouse desks to be picked up by the next person who touches that thing. The bacteria creates a toxin that generates the deadly symptoms. Fortunately, an antitoxin had been developed capable of stopping the progression. When Nome's Dr. Curtis Welch recognized what he was facing, after the deaths of a pair of children in mid-January, he realized the only way to avert an epidemic was to quarantine everyone exposed and inoculate the townspeople against the contagion as soon as humanly possible. The trouble: The hospital's supply of antitoxin serum had expired.

Though physically isolated by hundreds of miles of frozen tundra, Nome was connected to civilization by radio. The doctor first relayed the urgent need for a new supply of serum to Nome's mayor, George Maynard, and the town council, which instituted the quarantine. The plea for immediate aid was then sent out over the wires. The call reached Anchorage, Juneau, Seattle, and finally the US Public Health Service in Washington, D.C. The message: An epidemic was "almost inevitable." And the potential for mortality was catastrophic.

The first impulse of those on the receiving end of Nome's cry for help was to transport supplies of serum from the Lower 48 to the stricken town via aircraft. But the reality of winter's frigid temperatures quickly quashed that idea: The available airplanes had open cockpits, and pilots (not to mention instrumentation and mechanics) were sure to freeze. That didn't mean rescue by air lacked fierce advocates: The publisher of the *Fairbanks News-Miner*, William Fentress Thompson (also known as "Wrong Font" Thompson), maintained this was the best and quickest solution, and lobbied the territorial governor, Scott C. Bone, to give flying a try.

The alternative plan—one that involved feats of coordination—was to deliver the antitoxin by dogsled. While a massive shipment was culled from hospitals up and down the West Coast and shipped north, a supply discovered in the Anchorage Railroad Hospital could be dispatched immediately. Bone, charged with making the decision about mode of transport, weighed the pros and cons, and quickly opted for the tried and true: dogs and their mushers. About three hundred thousand units of serum were bundled in quilts and loaded onto a train, which carried cargo north to Nenana, at the confluence of the Nenana and Tanana Rivers, where the great serum run along the Iditarod Trail began.

In Nenana, the bundled serum was loaded onto the sled of mail carrier Bill Shannon, the first musher in the relay. He set off into the freezing sub-Arctic night, bound for the first transfer in Tolovana. Meantime, Leonhard Seppala, a Norwegian with a stellar reputation as a musher in Nome, set off with his team. Directing a team led by the soon-to-be legendary husky named Togo, Seppala was bound for the trail's midway point in Nulato, where he'd take up the load for his leg of the relay.

Over the next five days (plus a few hours), Nome's salvation was handed off from musher to musher, from frozen hand to warm, from exhausted team to fresh, traveling mile over wintry Alaskan mile. The mushers and the serum were wrapped in quilts and bearskins, but still the cold pierced. The mittens of Athabascan musher Edgar Kalland froze to his sled; when he arrived at the roadhouse where he'd make his transfer, a worker there had to pour hot water over the mitts to free him.

The dogs suffered too. Their masters took care to not drive them too hard when temperatures dipped toward sixty degrees below zero, knowing their lungs could freeze. Their undersides were protected from frostbite with rabbit skins, their paws enveloped in booties. They also displayed an instinctive sense of how to keep themselves, and their musher, safe on the hazardous and elusive trail. On one leg of the relay, the story goes, Charlie Evans encountered a ground fog so dense he could barely make out the dogs closest to his sled, much less the path forward. He was traveling along the Yukon River at that point, and sections of open water posed a serious hazard. The dogs, however, knew the way. The ability of huskies to suss out safe passage is legendary among mushers, and the best dogs are those who smell or sense danger and lead their teams away from it.

Musher Leonhard Seppala and his dogsled team.
CREATIVE COMMONS

That said, two of Evans's dogs would not survive their ordeal. Though the musher unhitched them and carried them the final distance to his endpoint, they would ultimately succumb to the cold.

Through blinding and relentless storms, the mushers and teams carried on. Leonhard Seppala and his Siberian huskies was still traveling toward his intended starting point in Nulato when he nearly passed Harry Ivanoff's team, which had the serum on board. The transfer was made amidst blowing snow, and Seppala, with Togo in the lead, wheeled around to retrace his tracks. His remarkable passage defied possibility, but it turned out what was possible had yet to be defined. Togo and the other dogs had ticked off forty miles before the rendezvous with Ivanoff; without rest, they now turned toward home. They had lives to save.

The team pushed on through a gale. Reaching the shore of Norton Bay, Seppala considered his options, weighing the pitfalls of travel across the potentially fractured ice against shaving precious miles, and time, off the run. Five more people had perished in Nome, and another thirty were thought to have the disease. He opted to cross the frozen water, and trusted Togo to find the way. The remarkable dog did just that.

When Seppala's team finally reached the end of their leg, they'd traveled farther than any other—nearly 261 miles, from Nome to Shaktoolik, where they picked up the package, then from Shaktoolik to Golovin, where they passed it on to Charlie Olson and his team. Olson powered on through the storm to meet the last relay in the settlement of Bluff. With the storied

Musher Gunnar Kaasen and Balto, the husky that led the last leg of the Great Serum Run to Nome.
Wiki Commons

Balto in the lead, musher Gunnar Kaasen logged fifty-three miles to the endpoint, a remarkable feat but a distant second to the distance covered by Seppala and his team.

A final drama confounded Kaasen and his dogs as they neared their destination, when a vicious wind flipped the sled and tumbled the huskies. Kaasen righted the vehicle, then checked to ensure the cargo was still secure . . . and discovered it was gone. For frantic moments in the dark and swirling snow, he searched among drifts for the serum with his bare hands, and finally recovered it. His fingers were frostbitten, but he was able to lash down the load and see it delivered safely.

When the second load of serum arrived in Anchorage, the relay was on again, with some of the same mushers ensuring the next batch of antitoxin also arrived safely in Nome. There were losses—both for families in the settlement and among the huskies who'd plowed through wicked winter weather to reach it. But the rescue was a success; with the serum in hand, Dr. Welch and his nurses were able to begin vaccinations, and the epidemic was averted.

In the months that followed, stories of the mushers' bravery and sacrifice spread, and praise and commendations were conferred. Territorial governor Scott Bone praised the "thirty-odd" men who participated in the historic runs in a letter to the editor of the Seattle Times, writing: "Heroism of the finest type was shown by these mushers and their dogs. Not an hour was unnecessarily lost and the responsive Alaskan spirit was displayed at its best."

The selfless motivation of mushers like Bill Shannon, Edgar Kalland, and Leonhard Seppala, as well as of people in the small communities who provided support across hundreds of miles of inhospitable terrain, has been paid forward into the ethos driving modern Alaskan rescues. Coming together to save lives no matter the challenge is the serum run's legacy, and a baseline for today's search and rescue.

Another serum run legacy is the modern Iditarod sled-dog race, an annual event celebrating the musher, the husky, and the tradition of sled-dog travel in the state. Dogsled races have a long history in Alaska, and in Nome. Leonhard Seppala sharpened both his knowledge of the region's trails and his dog-handling skills in the All Alaska Sweepstakes, according to one writer; this race traversed more than four hundred miles of lonely terrain surrounding the settlement and other sub-Arctic outposts in the early twentieth century. The sweepstakes were discontinued following World War I, but friendly competition among mushers carried on in other venues throughout the territory.

The love of sled dogs and the excitement of racing reached across the decades, but it wasn't until 1973 that the magic of the serum run story was incorporated. After years of effort and with the help of historian Dorothy Page and a host of other enthusiasts, Joe Redington was able to marry those legacies in the first modern Iditarod Trail Sled Dog Race. Following sections of the original serum run route (the course varies from year to year), competitors and their teams race from the Anchorage area all the way to Nome. The winner of that first race, a thirty-year-old gold miner named Dick Wilmarth, who reportedly secured five dogs for his team in a swap for a snow machine, completed the run in twenty days, forty-nine minutes, and forty-one seconds. In the years that have followed, the popularity of the event has grown, with the names of repeat winners like Susan Butcher and Lance Mackey making headlines around the world.

The spirit of rescue endures along the Iditarod as well. Even in competition, and into the most recent times, mushers look out for each other, and for their dogs. In 2018 musher Jim Lanier and his team were nearing Nome—on the last legs of the race—when a blizzard blew up. Wind spun the snow into a whiteout and temperatures plunged to sixty degrees below zero. Lanier lost sight of the trail markers in the swirling, drifting snow, heading off-course toward the Bering Sea. When he realized what had happened, Lanier attempted to get back on track. But the dogs became tangled in driftwood. They couldn't move.

By the time fellow musher Scott Janssen found him, Lanier was hypothermic. Janssen, owner of a funeral home and known as the "Mushing Mortician," raised the alarm via radio, then hunkered down with his comrade to wait. Neither men finished the race, but it didn't matter. What mattered was sticking together and supporting each other until help arrived.

Race organizers dispatched a snow machine, which transported both men off the trail and into medical care.

The dog teams also had to be rescued. Musher Mike Owens, a member of the Iditarod Trail Committee's board of directors, headed into the storm to see what he could do. After all, he told a reporter, "[A] musher's No. 1 concern is not for their own well being but for their dogs." When he reached the dogs they were "huddled up," curled into balls to conserve heat, and covered in snow. Owens rubbed their eyes and muzzles to stimulate them, then hitched them to a sled and drove them to Nome.

As you might expect, those involved in the rescue diffused credit, the "humble contest" in full play. Janssen deflected credit for helping save Lanier's life in a distinctly Iditarod way, as had the mushers of the serum run. "The truth?" he told a local news agency. "The real heroes were my dogs . . . They were the true heroes."

The Amazing Leon Crane

—————

I was sure glad to get back to civilization.... There
were times when I thought I'd never make it.
—LIEUTENANT LEON CRANE, QUOTED IN HIS HOMETOWN
NEWSPAPER, THE *PHILADELPHIA INQUIRER*, ON MARCH 17, 1944

Search and rescue. Survival and recovery. In the story of Leon Crane, SAR takes on uniquely Alaskan proportions. From the instigating spiral of a military aircraft to the forensics that brought about a semblance of closure, the chain of events is unlikely. Yet as the story of Crane and his colleagues unwinds, first over three months of an Alaskan winter and then over decades, it touches on both obvious and more subtle ways SAR manifests in the psyches of those living in the Far North.

In December 1943 Lieutenant Leon Crane was a twenty-four-year-old pilot stationed at Ladd Field in Fairbanks. The field had gone into service several years earlier as a site where the cold-weather operations of aircraft could be tested. Fairbanks in winter was—and continues to be—an ideal location for such tests: Temperatures in the region begin to plummet in October and lows average in the double digits below zero in the dark days of December, January, and February (the record low is a reported –66°F). The former gold-mining town is situated near the ecotone between sub-arctic boreal forest and arctic tundra, within sight of the mighty Alaska Range and Denali, the highest point on the North American continent. It offers challenging variables of terrain for training and testing, all regularly swept by gales and blizzards. With battle lines in World War II encompassing the high mountains of Europe and frigid Russia, understanding how an aircraft's instrumentation and mechanical components fared in such extremes was critical to the war effort.

Crane was copilot on a mission that departed on December 21; the plan was to test the propeller feathering system of a B-24 Liberator, a wartime workhorse her crew dubbed the *Iceberg Inez*. The five-man team also included pilot Lieutenant Harold Hoskin, Lieutenant James Sibert, Sergeant Ralph Wenz, and Master Sergeant Richard Pompeo. To complete the test, pilot Hoskin headed southeast from Fairbanks as planned, toward Big Delta at the confluence of the Tanana and Delta Rivers. But heavy cloud cover at that site precluded the required aerial maneuvers. Hoskin and Crane scanned the horizon seeking better weather conditions. A patch of lightening sky indicated a spot where they could carry out their assignment, and they strayed from the flight plan, heading northeast to take advantage of the break in the cloud cover.

When they encountered what Hoskin deemed an appropriate hole in the ceiling, the pilot arced the plane upward. But at about twenty-five thousand feet one of the four engines quit, and the aircraft began a dizzying downward spiral, one that Hoskin and Crane struggled to arrest. They were able to win a brief reprieve, but the pressures on the plane had compromised other systems, and the Liberator plunged into another dive. As the ground spun closer, Hoskin gave the order to bail out. In the chaos, and despite the confounding centrifugal forces, Crane was able to get his parachute on; Pompeo was able to do the same. As he tumbled through the bomb-bay doors, Crane noted Hoskin still getting into his chute. Then he was out, into the cold. He'd never see his crewmates again.

When the *Iceberg Inez* didn't return to base that day as planned, officers at Ladd Field immediately launched a rescue effort. The plane wasn't the first to go missing since the airfield had opened, and this wasn't the first search and rescue airmen stationed at the field had ever conducted. Even in winter, flyers had survived or been successfully rescued after their ships fell from the frozen skies. One of those included crewmate Richard Pompeo, who had been stationed in Alaska for several years and had survived a crash landing in an earlier north-country winter, when he and another flyer were forced down on a frozen river while attempting to

The wreckage of Leon Crane's B-24 Liberator rests on a hillside in Yukon-Charley Rivers National Preserve.
NATIONAL PARK SERVICE. PHOTO: JOSH SPICE

reach Whitehorse in Canada's Yukon Territory. They'd walked to shelter and safety.

But saving the crew of the *Iceberg Inez* would prove an impossible challenge for the soldiers and officers at Ladd. The plane wasn't anywhere near where it was supposed to be. The baseline reference for rescuers was the airship's last location, radioed in by Wenz. That starting point was Big Delta. In searching for a break in the weather, however, Hoskin had flown far afield, and both the spin and the attempted recovery added untraceable miles. Also, and unfortunately, Wenz hadn't kept up with protocol in keeping Ladd updated on the plane's coordinates. "If Wenz had kept to the schedule," writer Brian Murphy notes in *81 Days below Zero*, "there would have been a call to Ladd just before the B-24 went into its spin." That meant Big Delta was at least thirty minutes of flight time away from where the plane crashed, in any direction. The amount of ground rescuers would have to cover was daunting.

Add to that the weather variables—it was winter, after all. Under clear skies, pilots on aerial reconnaissance stood a chance of spotting the metal fuselage of a plane, which could catch the sun and stand out in contrast to the tundra and taiga. Another possibility: catching sight of smoke. Though it's not what any searcher wants to see, a plume rising from wreckage makes an excellent homing beacon.

Complications didn't deter officials at Ladd. An experienced Alaskan flyer, Major R. C. Ragle, was in charge of the SAR operation, and he knew what he was up against. The window for success was short—measured in days, given the season—so he responded in force. In his account of the search, writer Murphy notes that by December 23 "more than twenty search missions had been made from Ladd Field ... beginning about eight hours after the last radio contact with the *Iceberg Inez*."

But because the efforts were focused on Big Delta, the searchers had had no luck. The size of the Alaskan mile is just as prodigious from the air; the downed plane and its crew members were the proverbial needles in a sprawling snow-covered haystack. Another sixteen planes were scheduled to go up on December 24. The search radius was increased. Reconnaissance continued, day after short day. But it was all to no avail.

Ragle called off the effort about a week after the plane went down. In his report, he notes that between nine and seventeen aircraft had been dispatched daily in the search, without result. In Murphy's account, the major

Ladd Field in Fairbanks, as seen from the air circa 1942 during the Cold Weather Testing Mission.
COURTESY OF THE US ARMY VIA THE NATIONAL PARK SERVICE

declared flights over the Big Delta region went on "until no reasonable chance existed that further search would locate the missing aircraft."

Ragle also speculated that the plane could have been pushed northward by prevailing winds, and that Hoskin could have touched her down somewhere near the Yukon River, where he and the crew were "safe and comfortably supplied and encamped." If that was the case, it was possible that even though the search was called off, the flyers could still be rescued. Nothing more could be done, but he held out hope.

The most compelling prong of Crane's SAR story is his self-rescue. After the crash, he could have curled into a ball of hopelessness and given up. But personal resilience and good luck conspired in his favor. His reserves—emotional, physical, intellectual—were extraordinary, given the circumstances. He survived the next eighty-four days alone in the wilderness.

The young flier, who'd only been stationed in Alaska for about five months before the accident, hit the ground with no survival equipment save the clothes on his back, his silk parachute, a pocketknife, a handful of matches, and a letter from his father, which he would use as tinder. His limited experience in the extremes of Alaskan winters was a mixed blessing. He knew some of the dangers he faced: frostbite, for example. In the rush to bail out of the doomed Liberator, he'd forgotten to put on his mittens. He'd have to take special care to ensure his fingers didn't freeze. On the flip side, there were hundreds of other ways he could die. He'd discover them the hard way.

In the first hours and days after the crash, Crane did what every competent person lost in any wilderness awaiting rescue should do. He built an SOS out of tree boughs, knowing his comrades from Ladd were looking for him. He hailed the crew of the *Iceberg Inez*, shouting their names to the sky, but no one answered. He set up a makeshift camp next to a stream, ensuring he had access to water. He wrapped himself in the insulation of his parachute, built and nurtured a fire, and then huddled close to fend off the penetrating chill. He attempted to hunt squirrels, with no success. He conserved his strength as best he could. He stayed put. He waited, but no one came.

After nine days, recognizing he was too far off the search grid and rescue was not an option—not to mention he was starving and freezing—the airman was spurred to action. He set out on the first leg of a long, dangerous walk, doing his best to figure out which way to go on a completely foreign landscape. When he encountered the Charley River, he not only wasn't sure what river he was on but also which way to turn. Frostbitten but determined, he headed north.

That's when he got lucky, and when an Alaskan tradition also came into play. Rounding a river bend, he encountered trapper Phil Berail's cabin and cache. Berail, like other trappers along the Charley River and elsewhere throughout Alaska, had stocked the cabin with survival supplies for travelers who found themselves in dire straits in an inhospitable wilderness—travelers like Crane. The trekker downed some raisins, lit a fire, and took stock. The cabin contained everything he needed to rebuild his strength, from bags of rice, beans, sugar, and flour to mukluks (traditional footwear), long underwear, a rifle, and moose-hide mittens. Maybe the cabin's owner would return and bring him home. If not, Crane had what he needed to carry on.

Crane spent the next few days eating, defrosting his extremities, and figuring out how best to move forward, since it became clear the cabin's owner was probably not coming back until spring or summer. He made a couple of aborted trips along the river on foot, but quickly realized he couldn't carry enough supplies on his back to see him through. Using Berail's stores and tools, he fashioned a sledge and rigged it so he could haul it. In mid-February, the sound of ice breaking up on the Charley inspired Crane to speed up his plans to seek out civilization, since the river was his highway. He outfitted himself in the gear he'd need to stave off the bitter cold and loaded the sledge with enough food and supplies to support a long haul, including the rifle and ammunition. Then he set out, hoping the frozen river would lead him to salvation.

The next leg of the journey presented another set of challenges and uncertainties. As the planet slowly tipped toward spring, the river ice became more unpredictable. Several times the heavy sled punctured the surface. Crane knew if the sled went under, his lifeline was lost … and because he was hitched to it, there was a good chance he'd be lost, too, sucked into water that would bring on hypothermia in moments. When that finally happened—the sled broke through and dragged the pilot toward the breach—Crane was able to haul himself and his gear to safety. He dried off, took a breather, and carried on. Fortunately, he didn't have far to travel before reaching another trapper's cabin, which offered him a chance to restock and regroup.

But in early March, the melting ice got the better of Crane's sled. This time it went all the way in, and Crane went most of the way in with it. Murphy describes tense moments as Crane clawed his way out of the Charley's freezing flow, then succeeded in getting the sledge back onto solid ice as well. Again, he dried off and took stock. As far as the sled was concerned, Crane decided "the river had won." He headed back to the last trapper's cabin and repacked, this time carrying what he needed on his back in a pack.

On March 9, Crane encountered a makeshift runway for bush pilots lined with spruce boughs, and a set of tracks leading into the woods. The next day he followed the tracks to another trapper's cabin—this one inhabited. Drying clothes fluttered on a clothesline. The airman was, by all accounts, astounded and overjoyed. He hollered, and the trapper opened the cabin door.

Crane presented a frightening countenance. In his own words: "I had a two-inch beard, black as coal; my hair was long and matted, covering my ears and coming down over my forehead almost to my eyes, so that I looked like some strange species of prehistoric man. I was dirty and sunburned and wind-burned, and my eyes stared back at me from the centers of two deep black circles."

But Albert Ames and his family welcomed the weary traveler. After he was warmed, fed, and rested, Ames and Crane set out for the outpost of Woodchopper, where there was a radio and an airfield. Woodchopper was also home to Phil Berail, whose cache and cabin had saved the airman's life; the two men met there and swapped stories before a bush pilot named Bob Rice flew in. Rice was Crane's escort out of the wilderness, and back to Ladd Field.

Lieutenant Leon Crane participated in a recovery mission to the crash of his B-24 after surviving a long solo trek through the Alaskan wilderness.
NATIONAL PARK SERVICE; COURTESY OF UNIVERSITY OF ALASKA ANCHORAGE ARCHIVES, LEON CRANE COLLECTION

Crane's incredible survival story made headlines across the United States, but once the brouhaha quieted down, the airman let the tale slip quietly into history. He penned a single account of his long trek and survival, published in 1944. After that, even when asked, writers note he'd politely decline to discuss the crash or its aftermath. In the spirit of the "humble contest," Crane went forward with his life like nothing remarkable had happened.

The last prong of the Crane SAR story is the recovery of his lost crew-mates. The military is tenacious about bringing home their fallen and finding their missing in action. With Crane's help and direction, the bodies of Lieutenant Sibert and Sergeant Wenz were found and retrieved in the spring of 1944. In that search, no sign of Hoskin and Pompeo could be found.

But they were never forgotten.

Decades passed, and the remote crash site on the tundra retained its secrets. When it became part of Yukon-Charley Rivers National Preserve in 1980, however, things changed. More than a hundred million acres of Alaskan wilderness were set aside in national parks and preserves in that year, the product of a hotly contested piece of legislation known as the Alaska National Interest Lands Conservation Act (ANILCA). This sweeping new law established the National Park Service as caretaker of nearly 2.5 million acres of tundra, mountain, and river basin surrounding the confluence of the Yukon and Charley Rivers, including the Liberator's crash site. The park service has a dual purpose—to preserve and protect the nation's wildlands, and also to make them accessible to the public. In the case of the Yukon-Charley preserve, remoteness precludes the kind of visitation that most national parks must contend with. But it doesn't preclude interpretation, which enhances the public's understanding of the region's natural and cultural history.

Crane's remarkable survival story was part of that history, as was the mystery surrounding the fate of Hoskin and Pompeo. In 1994 park service historian Douglas Beckstead was employed in the Yukon-Charley preserve and fascinated by the mystery of the B-24's disappearance. He first saw the remains of the *Iceberg Inez* from the air as a passenger aboard a helicopter. Murphy describes the sight this way:

> *Below, shining in the same metallic hues as the river, was the resting place of the B-24D, whose paint had been burned away by the fire in the crash. Decades of subarctic weather scrubbed away whatever was left, leaving only the gleaming raw steel and other metal. . . . The nose of the* Iceberg Inez *and its two*

inner engines were shattered and scattered as if lopped off with a giant hammer. Other parts of the wings, incredibly, withstood the impact. Some of the wing lines were as sharp and clean as the day the plane left Ladd Field. But two huge spaces—like missing teeth in a smile—were gouged out from the wings when the outer engines ripped away. The steel propeller blades, dinged and scarred from slicing into the rocks, stood like sentinels on the edge of the debris field.

Over the next decades, Beckstead compiled a vast store of information about the incident and Crane's remarkable journey—"notes, documents, and 25,000 photographs" culled from interviews, military records, and other sources. He'd also returned to the site over the years, retrieving artifacts, including a parachute buckle, which Beckstead told one writer was "the first clue that the plane went down with Hoskin still in it." He even retrieved bone fragments, which Murphy notes the historian sent to the military, "believing they could be human remains. They weren't."

In 2006 a military forensics team with the Joint POW/MIA Accounting Command began excavations at the crash site. They uncovered small artifacts that hinted at the identities of the plane's occupants: watch bodies, buckles, key rings, pocketknives . . . and more bone fragments. All the evidence was sent to a lab, where anthropologists and other experts set about trying to discover the identities of those who'd left the items behind. They determined the bones belonged to pilot Harold Hoskin. The remains of Ladd's fallen flyer were returned to his family and laid to rest at Arlington National Cemetery.

The remains of Richard Pompeo, however, still rest somewhere in the Yukon-Charley National Preserve. Perhaps yet another search and recovery will provide closure to his story.

The Good Friday Quake

In time of need when a good friend and neighbor requires and requests
a Helping Hand it is only natural to assist in every way possible.
—FROM THE REPORT TITLED "OPERATION HELPING HAND:
THE ARMED FORCES REACT TO EARTHQUAKE DISASTER"

On March 27, 1964, two of the planet's tectonic plates shifted abruptly, remodeling Southcentral Alaska. Far below Prince William Sound, the Pacific Plate gave way to the North American Plate, diving toward the molten sea of rock separating the planet's core from its shattered eggshell crust. The megathrust earthquake that resulted ranks as one of the strongest ever recorded along the infamous Pacific Ring of Fire.

The quake demolished Anchorage. A neighborhood overlooking the Turnagain Arm slid toward the sea. Downtown, roadways heaved and subsided; the buildings that lined them dropped, tilted, and crumbled. Along the Alaska Railroad, which links Anchorage to Seward in the south and Fairbanks in the north, tracks jumped free of their ties and came to rest in twisted heaps. The asphalt highway running alongside the railway splintered as well, cutting off the slender connections between Alaska's biggest city and smaller towns along the sound.

Those smaller towns, closer to the epicenter, also suffered significant damage in the tremor, but that was only the beginning of their disasters. The quake conjured tsunami waves that inundated the ports of Seward, Valdez, Whittier, and Kodiak. Most of the lives lost on that Good Friday were taken by the seismic waves, which swept victims relentlessly out to sea.

The magnitude 9.2 quake, which began at 5:36 p.m. and lasted four to five wrenching minutes, and the tsunamis that followed claimed 131 lives in Alaska. More lives were lost when sea waves swept along the Pacific Coast as far south as California. The quake remains the strongest ever recorded in North America, and the second strongest worldwide. In some places the earth subsided; in others it was uplifted, with the displacement measured in feet, not inches. The seafloor at Cape Cleare, on Montague Island in Prince William Sound, was upthrust a record ten meters (more than thirty-two feet), with marine life lifted out of reach of high tide, where it perished, creating a beach where there had been none before, and coating it in white skeletons. By contrast, the village of Portage, southeast of Anchorage on the shallowing Turnagain Arm, subsided as much as eight feet. Fissures split the ground like crevasses on a glacier, some thousands of feet long and yawning twenty feet wide. The heights of the deadly tsunamis that swept into seaside towns as far south as Crescent City, California, reached thirty to fifty feet, and moved at speeds up to five hundred miles per hour. The tallest wave, triggered by an undersea landslide (as were others, setting off what are called local sea waves), towered more than two hundred feet.

The nomenclature of earthquake classification would be revised to describe what occurred along the two-thousand-mile-long hinge in the crust below the Gulf of Alaska: megathrust. The US Army historian who recorded the effects of the quake at Elmendorf Air Force Base near Anchorage compared the forces released in terms of weaponry, noting the "earth tremor unleashed 200,000 megatons of energy, more than 2,000 times the power of the mightiest nuclear bomb ever detonated and 400 times the total of all nuclear bombs ever exploded..."

Considering the rupture's destructive power, it's a wonder more didn't perish. A few of the 131 Alaskan victims were killed when their homes or businesses collapsed. A few disappeared in landslides like the one that devastated the neighborhood of Turnagain Heights, where, according to the US Geological Survey, "an area of about 130 acres was devastated by displacements that broke the ground into many deranged blocks that were collapsed and tilted at all angles." The Turnagain slide carried seventy-five

The scene on Fourth Street in Anchorage following the Good Friday quake.
COURTESY OF US GEOLOGICAL SURVEY

homes onto the mudflats of the Cook Inlet, hundreds of feet below. The bulk of the casualties were swept out to sea by tsunami.

But there were plenty of survivors, and both quake and sea wave left many in need. A natural disaster so huge and extraordinary required a search-and-rescue operation of equal size and strength.

Throughout Southcentral Alaska in the immediate aftermath of the event, people starting reaching out to each other, consoling each other, rescuing each other. These SARs were impromptu. Neighbors scrambled down newly created bluffs to pluck children stranded on a car that had ridden the landslide in Turnagain Heights. Engineers from Elmendorf rigged a crane to free two men from the rubble of the control tower at Anchorage International Airport, which had collapsed and killed one man. In downtown Anchorage, a soldier from Fort Richardson watched a slab peel off the (JC) Penney building and flatten a Chevy parked in the street. A woman was trapped inside. "When the world stopped shaking," he said, "I called some people and we tried to lift the slab of concrete from the car." A bystander with a torch was finally able to cut through enough of the car's door to enable the rescuers to free the woman, who somehow, miraculously, survived.

More coordinated search-and-rescue efforts organized just as quickly. As soon as the buildings stopped shaking, the US Army Alaska, known as USARAL, mobilized for action, setting up a center of operations as well as a chain of command. Operation Helping Hand, a rescue and assistance effort considered "unparalleled" in Alaskan history, was underway.

That the military would take the lead in search and rescue after the earthquake seemed only natural. The army, air force, and navy personnel stationed in the territory had an established infrastructure for SAR, its history dating back to the territory's frontier days and consolidated in wartime. But before servicemen and -women could deploy they assessed damages to their own, following the advice given by flight attendants: Put on your own oxygen mask before helping others put on theirs. Elmendorf, located a few miles north of downtown Anchorage, and Fort Richardson, next door to the northeast, had sustained relatively minor damage compared to locales within the city. That's not to say the bases were unscathed, or that the people working there didn't experience extraordinary events. One soldier at Fort Richardson suffered head injuries from falling debris; he later died, reportedly the only casualty among Alaska's armed forces. Elmendorf's air traffic control tower was so badly damaged it was unusable. Across both base and fort, windows shattered and masonry crumbled. Significantly, the water supply from Ship Creek was interrupted when the earth moved upstream from the reservoir, blocking the flow.

But both Elmendorf and Fort Richardson were situated on relatively stable ground, and the hardships faced by those who lived and worked there paled by comparison to those faced by residents just a few miles distant and in the seaside towns soldiers would be dispatched to in the days and weeks that followed.

SAR was the first order of business for Operation Helping Hand. Troops fanned out into Anchorage and surrounding communities, doing their best to stabilize shaky buildings and comfort an uncertain populace. Alaska's largest city, Anchorage—at the time, home to more than fifty thousand people—was described by a reporter as having been "shaken and clawed by monster hands," with fissures "like zigzagging lines of black lightning" ripped through streets, yards, and structures. "Many buildings and private homes lay in dismal ruin, some in holes where there had been no holes before, others heaved up onto ridges where there had been no ridges before."

The marquee of the Denali Theater rests on the sidewalk after the Good Friday quake.
COURTESY OF US GEOLOGICAL SURVEY

A detachment of 125 troops and their commanders worked to secure the downtown area. A "specially trained mountain rescue team" from Fort Richardson was dispatched to the Turnagain area, but before they were deployed, officers reconnoitered in the area. They found the road leading to the neighborhood "ended abruptly in a 25-foot cliff." Below, houses lay in a jumbled mess, an area three blocks wide and about six blocks long having been "scrambled in an insane fashion by the earth tremors." Given the impending darkness, instability of any anchors, the threat of tsunami, and the fact that, given seven hours had passed since the initial shock, most survivors had already been transported to safety, the officers decided to hold their men back.

The Anchorage Public Safety Building became a central point of contact for the military and civilians, while the "beehive center" was the USARAL Operations Center. No task was too menial, even for men higher up the chain of command—colonels were armed with staplers to keep paperwork in order. Anchorage's city government, the Salvation Army, the Red Cross, mountaineers, ski clubs, mushers, and a small army of otherwise unaffiliated civilians collaborated on a variety of fronts to make sure victims had what they needed, from typhoid shots for the homeless and generators for local hospitals to clean drinking water and radio equipment so that messages could be broadcast to loved ones outside the disaster area. Four

The twisted tracks of the Alaska Railroad testify to the earthquake's strength.
COURTESY OF US GEOLOGICAL SURVEY

water purification stations were set up, since the city's water supply was compromised. Four "mess halls" were established to feed those who'd been displaced. Emergency housing was provided at Elmendorf, sheltering as many as two thousand evacuees over time.

Conditions on the ground made overland transportation sketchy; and weather made rescue by air difficult. But on March 29, under clearing skies, USARAL deployed twenty-two airships, which logged "71.1 hours, made 91 sorties, transported 105 passengers and 4,905 pounds of cargo, and rescued 6 persons." The sorties involved supply runs, photographic missions to document damages, delivery of heavy-equipment operators and specialists (such as bulldozer operators and communications special-ists to establish contact with the port of Whittier), and ferrying the press, which arrived in force following news of the disaster. Humanitarian flights would continue, whenever conditions allowed, for the duration of Opera-tion Helping Hand.

As reports of devastation trickled in from Seward, Whittier, Kodiak, and Valdez, all coastal communities bulldozed by sea waves in the wake of the temblor, the reach of Operation Helping Hand expanded. On the day following the quake, a pilot evacuating a husband, wife, and their deceased baby, who'd been killed in Whittier, spotted a group of people on the Seward

Highway near Portage. They'd been trapped overnight by landslides that took out the road behind and ahead. Sixteen women and children were loaded onto the plane and flown to Anchorage. A woman in labor was airlifted to the hospital; when that helicopter arrived on the site, an army historian reported that "practically everyone in the area came running with their entire belongings, wanting to be evacuated." The pilot had to refuse all but the most urgent requests, as there was simply no room aboard the airship.

Over those first days, weather permitting, soldiers and civilians flew over and into settlements to both assess damage and offer assistance to survivors. They harbored their resources carefully. The initial report from the port of Whittier, hard hit by both quake and tsunami, was that the town was entirely aflame. But a bit later, the highway patrol reported that the railroad and automobile tunnel through Maynard Mountain, which connected the town to Anchorage and other settlements on the Kenai Peninsula, was open. Fifteen residents were safe, one was confirmed dead, one was injured, and twelve were missing, carried away by the sea wave that destroyed the docks. But the survivors had supplies and shelter. The fire was confined to the port's oil tanks. USARAL officials, committed to deploying resources where they were most needed, "postponed any immediate action concerning the Port of Whittier and turned their attention to more pressing problems in other devastated areas. There would be time later to tidy up the debris at Whittier."

The port of Valdez was also washed away by a tsunami, as were thirty-two of its residents, and three people were confirmed dead. Survivors were shell-shocked. In an Operation Helping Hand report, the writer states the town had "taken a desperate beating. The waterfront was a tangle of smashed timbers, boats, and debris of all sorts." Its oil tank farm, like Whittier's, was ablaze. The devastation, coupled with still-present dangers, prompted the mayor to issue an evacuation order. An evacuation center was set up at Gulkana. The Glennallen High School, located about 120 miles north of Valdez, had only minor damage and, with the help of the school's custodian, was also outfitted as an evacuation center. Recognizing the town site's vulnerability, and unwilling to risk a replay of the disaster, Valdez would eventually be relocated to higher ground.

In Seward, an army private was enjoying his supper in the mess hall when the quake struck. Outside, a train with new cars was parked on the waterside rail line. "It gets tossed into the water like nothing," he said afterward. "The whole train just gets flipped into the water and the bridge it was on was gone and the tracks are hopping like rubber bands." Then the sea wave hit. Another port washed away, another fire in town, another population in shock and need.

Likewise the village of Chenega, located on an island in the southwest reaches of Prince William Sound. The settlement was essentially erased by tsunami, leaving survivors huddled on the high ground with only the clothes on their backs and the supplies stored in a hilltop schoolhouse. They all were eventually evacuated by air.

In Kodiak, fourteen people died and $24 million in damages to boats, homes, and businesses was tallied. Following the quake and subsequent seismic wave, more than 200 people left the island, and another 270 were forced to leave their homes in town and seek shelter in outlying villages.

In all these places, as soon as humanly possible, helpers were on the way or immediately in play, often in the form of troops. Twenty-one soldiers were stationed in Seward when the earthquake struck; they joined civilians in searching for the missing and injured, establishing evacuation centers, and clearing debris. The Civil Air Patrol sprang into action, delivering tons of food—and the volunteers to distribute and serve it—to Seward and other towns on the Kenai cut off by damaged roads and tsunami-ravaged ports.

As the missing were accounted for and the immediate needs of survivors were met, the focus of Operation Helping Hand turned to recovery. Starting in April, and stretching through the short Alaskan summer, soldiers removed the rubble of collapsed buildings in downtown Anchorage and in Turnagain Heights. To facilitate access to seaside towns cut off by landslides, broken asphalt, and twisted rail lines, the army helped clear the Richardson Highway. Troops erected Bailey bridges to put the Seward Highway back into operation; seventeen spans were damaged or destroyed between Anchorage and the port town. And they erected telephone poles,

In Whittier, hard hit by tsunami following the 1964 quake, a survivor examines a tire pierced by a plank, evidence of the wave's force.
COURTESY OF US GEOLOGICAL SURVEY

which enabled rescuers and relief workers, as well as families and friends, to reconnect over miles of Alaskan wilderness and with loved ones in the Lower 48.

An astonishing force of aircraft and personnel was mobilized for the duration of Operation Helping Hand. By the time the effort wound down, in early May 1964, more than one hundred aircraft—C-124s, C-123s, C-130s were the workhorses, but other fixed-wing airships and helicopters were used—had taken to the skies, moving people to safety and supplies to where they were needed most desperately. By one count, 1,850 tons of gear, including generators, water purification and construction equipment, and personal items (clothing, toiletries), were shuttled around the Southcentral. Pilots logged more than thirteen hundred hours in the air. Doctors, nurses, construction workers, and other support personnel—nearly one thousand people—were also moved via air, with more still traveling to the needy overland or by water.

⚬⚬

More than thirty years later, Donald L. Darnell of Kodiak wrote a potent essay about the waves that washed away much of his hometown in the wake of the quake. Founded by Russian colonialists in the late eighteenth century, Kodiak has a checkered geologic history: Darnell recounts that the native First People advised the founders not to build on the site, as it had been taken out by earthquakes and tidal waves in earlier times. The town was also blanketed in feet of ash following the eruption of Novarupta in 1912; that eruption created the Valley of Ten Thousand Smokes, now preserved in Katmai National Park and Preserve. What had happened before was destined to happen again.

But Darnell's Kodiak is a stubborn place. The town's hardcore drunks refused to leave the bar even as the sea waves rolled in higher and higher, and thousands of whiskey bottles were found in the post-quake and tsunami debris. Unlike in Valdez, where the town was relocated wholesale from the now-known tsunami danger zone, Kodiak's town fathers opted to bring in eight feet of gravel and rebuild on the same site. Like nothing ever happened.

These days, after more than fifty years, visitors to the ports and towns rocked by the Good Friday quake would see no outward sign of the upheaval. The landscape's remodeling has become familiar. Where uplift and subsidence occurred, where fissures opened and closed, the contours of relocated coastlines, are now simply part of the terrain.

But the earth doesn't stop shifting. On November 30, 2018, a powerful quake rocked Southcentral Alaska. The temblor was pegged at 7.0, many degrees of magnitude less than the Good Friday quake, but significant nonetheless. The upheaval, both in terms of the land and the people, was also significant. Photographs capture images of jumbled roadways, cars perched precariously on blocks of asphalt separated by chasms. A video shot in an Anchorage courtroom captures the amazing length of the event, a sampling of the damage done to the building and to the peace of mind of the two women who took shelter under desks.

A tsunami warning was issued, but no tsunami materialized. The quake occurred along a different fault line; this was no megathrust disaster. No one perished, though plenty of damage to buildings, roadways, and other infrastructure occurred. There were plenty of differences, but one thing was the same—the helping hand. In the days that followed, as aftershocks rocked the region, folks in Anchorage, Eagle Creek, Joint Base Elmendorf-Richardson, Wasilla, and communities between came together to support each other.

Reporter Madeline McGee of the *Anchorage Daily News* had only been on the job—in the state, for that matter—for two weeks when the quake struck. She described a train rolling through her apartment, a section of roadway that "looked as though God had reached down and punched it," fires and power outages and floods.

But she also witnessed something remarkable. Within a week, towns and cities throughout Mat-Su Borough were getting back to normal. "Alaska accomplished an infrastructure feat I didn't know was possible," she wrote. "Five days after the equivalent of 199,000 tons of TNT rocked the region, the roads are passable. The water is clean. The gas has stopped leaking. The trains are running. The school system is about to reopen.... Alaskans have picked themselves up and moved on with what looks to be barely a stumble."

Moreover, she witnessed the helping hand. People mopping up, taking neighbors in, offering whatever resources they had to one another. Her gratitude spills onto the page: "Since Friday, lots of people have wryly told me, 'Welcome to Alaska.' In a way, though, this is a better welcome than most. It's only been a month, and I've already seen an enormous spectrum of uniquely Alaskan fortitude. And more importantly, I've seen how dependent that fortitude is on community and love. Welcome to Alaska, indeed."

Even without the 2018 jolt, and the plethora of aftershocks that kept locals on their toes throughout the city and beyond, Anchorage remembers. In the once-devastated Turnagain Heights neighborhood, west and south of the central city, a parcel has been set aside as Earthquake Park. In early spring, on the trails along the waterfront, the cold air bites and the trails are snow covered. The woodland hides the wounds, with spruce and birch pushing against paths that wind down toward the tide line, passing interpretive signs that tell the scientific parts of the story, the ones that describe what an earthquake does and the forces that drive upheaval. On the monument at the overlook, scant mention is made of the human trauma and the helping hand. A coastal trail intersects; turn one direction and a walker transects the slide path; turn the other, and that same walker sees only whispering forest and rippled gray sea. Alaska remembers.

The Mixed Blessing of the Machine

———

Outside cities like Anchorage and Fairbanks, native Alaskans can live off the land much as they have for thousands of years. It's called subsistence, which has a dire ring, but today's First People, like their ancestors, are adept at harvesting Alaska's bounty—salmon, caribou, berries, sea mammals—a wealth that has sustained them even through the onslaught of colonization. Knowledge and adaptation accumulated through generations support the subsistence lifestyles of Athabascans in the Interior, Iñupiats in the Arctic, Tlingit in the Southeast, and others. Colonial emigrants from Russia, and then North America, have appropriated native skills over time, and despite challenges presented by growing populations and declining resources, these days Alaskans of all backgrounds may choose to live exclusively by subsistence, or incorporate aspects of subsistence into their modern lifestyles.

In generations past, subsistence involved nomadic movement along traditional trails via kayak or dogsled. These human- or animal-powered conveyances have since given way to vehicles with motors—boats, float planes, automobiles (where roads are present), and snow machines. Search and rescue on waterways is the subject for another book, and your average motorcar mostly doesn't go missing, as it's generally confined to well-traveled thoroughfares (at least by Alaskan standards).

Snow machines and aircraft are another matter. Flying from outpost to outpost in a small plane is a travel staple, with a small army of skilled bush pilots ferrying people and supplies reliably and safely, provided the weather and equipment cooperates. Planes and helicopters are also a staple in the SAR armamentarium, the best tools for locating the missing and transporting them to safety—again, provided it's not too cold or stormy, or things don't break down.

Snow machines present a conundrum, however. Filling the tank of a snow machine is easier than maintaining a sled-dog team, so machines replacing dogs as a preferred mode of travel is understandable. That said, proponents of sled dogs still argue teams of huskies are perfectly suited to travel in Alaska's bush. Their carburetors don't freeze up. They have a sixth sense about conditions—stories pepper Alaskan literature of dogs refusing to cross rivers with unstable ice or to venture out into lethal subzero temperatures. A snowmobile doesn't discern. So long as it starts, it goes. It's up to the operator to make decisions. And in Alaska, the consequences of operator error can be dire.

SNOW MACHINES

Freeze-up, in October and November, is an "awkward time" for those hoping to travel by snow machine. Ditto breakup, in April and May. River ice, glacial ice, and sea ice throughout the Interior, on the North Slope, and in the Southwest and Southcentral regions may look solid, but in fact may be undercut by currents and thinned by warming temperatures. A riverbed may be a reliable highway in January, but in spring or fall stability may be compromised, and breaking through can be deadly.

Freeze-up presents an additional hazard. Rescuers tell tales of travelers making their way to a basketball game or a birthday party in a neighboring village and having their snow machines bind up in forming pack ice, stranding them in freezing temperatures. Couple that with inadequate provisioning—the cowling on a snow machine is warm, so riders may not dress adequately for conditions, and the village may be along a route so well known the driver doesn't feel a need to carry emergency supplies—and search and rescue becomes search and recovery.

The alcohol factor also must be considered. Many Alaskans, in particular natives, have limited tolerance for liquor. Losing the way while under the influence is bad news, but if a wrong turn is followed by a

In winter, moving between villages, heading to hunting grounds, or seeking recreation means traveling long distances by snow machine.
PHOTO: TRACY SALCEDO

breakdown—or worse, a breakdown in a storm with inadequate clothing—the consequences can be life threatening.

In considering the conundrum of the snow machine, rescuers also note the mixed blessing of speed combined with distance. Snowmobiles allow backcountry travelers, including hunters, to travel farther into the bush than they could when sled dogs served as winter's cabbies. The animals' endurance, though prodigious, imposed limits on distance and, in SAR terms, search radius. When miles per gallon and a full tank of gas dictate the limits, snowmobilers may quickly find themselves in unfamiliar territory. Should a storm blow in, obscuring tracks, the sun, and the stars, way-finding may become impossible. A GPS unit with fully charged batteries doesn't offer any consolation if you can't plow through the drifts packed on a breadcrumb trail fifty miles long.

Each year, Alaskan newspapers contain stories, often brief and tragic, of men and women who head off on their machines for a visit, to go hunting, or just for fun, and simply disappear. A twenty-two-year-old man set off from Koyuk with a friend and vanished after they became separated; searchers recovered his snow machine using drag hooks in Norton Bay. A beloved brother from Wasilla fell behind his snowmobiling companions and vanished; after four days troopers were forced to call the search off, their efforts hampered by weather that kept their helicopter grounded, and snow conditions—twenty-eight inches fell during the search window—that bogged down their own snow machines. A nine-year-old boy out with his dad exploring in the Hoodoo Mountains disappeared into a "moulin"—a hole in a glacier where water had compromised the ice. Troopers, climbers from the North American Outdoor Institute, and members of the US Army's Black Rapids high-angle rescue team responded to the scene, but all they could spot in the crevasse was the child's helmet and goggles, and part of the vehicle he was riding.

In other cases, snow machiners themselves create the crises that set off search-and-rescue efforts. That was the case in March 1999, when clear weather and ample snow drew more than a hundred snowmobilers to Turnagain Pass, located about fifty-five miles southeast of Anchorage along the Seward Highway.

Avalanche conditions were hazardous on that early spring day. Several slopes in the popular winter sports area slid in the morning and early afternoon, one nearly catching a pair of snowmobilers in what's known as the powder blast—a forceful burst of air and snow dust pushed ahead of the main avalanche—but leaving them unharmed. By late afternoon another group, acknowledging the instability of the conditions, decided to call it quits, but not until they enjoyed one last hill-climbing hurrah.

Highmarking, where riders skim up mountainsides to the highest point possible, is a well-known avalanche trigger. In this case, the group's highmarking contest set off a massive avalanche. A slab six to seven feet deep broke across a slope a half mile across, running nearly a mile downhill and dropping nearly 1,750 feet, moving at eighty to a hundred miles per hour. A number of snowmobilers were caught in the slide and powder blast;

some escaped by outrunning it, others were carried by the flow, and still more were buried. An accident report acknowledges that the exact number of people who were caught in the slide or barely escaped would never be known.

The rescue effort was as massive as the slide. Witnesses were the first to respond, spreading across the debris field to extricate those they could locate. The first officials on the scene were Alaska State Troopers and firefighters from Girdwood, the nearby resort town and home of the Alyeska Ski Resort. They were soon joined by searchers from the National Ski Patrol, Chugach Powder Guides, the Alaska Mountain Rescue Group, Alaska Search and Rescue Dogs, the US Forest Service, and others. Helicopters helped transport rescuers to the scene. And more snow machines were put into service—nearly a hundred of them—ferrying equipment, food, and people to the site of the disaster.

Rescue efforts were limited by daylight and dangerous conditions in the immediate aftermath of the event, but the next day more than 200 people were mobilized. Nine teams of searchers with ten-foot-long probes scoured the debris field. At the height of the rescue effort, by one account, 450 people were working the accident site. Deteriorating weather conditions hampered rescue and recovery efforts over the week following the incident, and eventually officials were forced to call it off. But all the snow machiners caught in the slide were accounted for, including the six young men who lost their lives in the incident, recovered from icy tombs as deep as seven feet.

Analysis of the successes and shortcomings of the rescue effort illustrates the willingness of those involved in SAR to examine and reexamine how they approach different situations. In this case, rescuers contemplated why the snow machines were carried farther downslope by the avalanche than the riders; this didn't jibe with previous experience. Metal detectors, magnetometers, and other devices proved useless in this case, as did avalanche rescue dogs, because the scale of the slide was so massive. The shortcomings of using probe poles were also noted, and attributed to the inexperience of the searchers using them, the density of the avalanche debris, and other factors.

Despite the potential downsides—the person who drives into the unknown and never returns, or drives to a mountaintop and sets off a devastating chain of events—snow machines remain one of the best tools in the search-and-rescue kit. They're as critical to the successes of troopers and volunteers as a good satellite phone and the proper outerwear—items every snow machiner should be outfitted with at all times.

AIRSHIPS

The best Alaskan bush pilots have reputations as solid and storied as the best Alaskan mountaineers. Their bravest flights couple mad skills with insanity: takeoffs and landings on the unpaved, unfriendly surfaces of glaciers, lakes, tundra, and rivers, at altitudes unheard of, on bush airstrips like scratches on the landscape, in weather like fury.

And the same names are reverentially mentioned again and again in particular locales. Think Don Sheldon on Denali: Back in the day, he was the guy you wanted to fly you to base camp on the Kahiltna Glacier, and the guy you wanted to get you off the mountain—or drop you supplies—if you ran into trouble.

Based in Talkeetna, a "quaint little drinking town with a climbing problem" and air taxi central during Denali's climbing season, Sheldon's career as a bush pilot of extraordinary skill and fearlessness was solidified in 1958 when the flier, then thirty-six years old, executed a mind-boggling rescue in Devil's Canyon on the Susitna River. The Big Su presents itself as a relatively typical Alaskan waterway as it flows through the little town, gathering in the Chulitna and Talkeetna Rivers just upstream of Main Street and carrying them to the sea. But a notorious crimp in the riverbed lies upstream, where the Big Su is constricted into a single channel, generating Class VI rapids—rated "extraordinarily difficult" and conjuring unavoidable storm surge–style waves that evoke seasickness in video, and mayhem in real life.

Devil's Canyon already had a long reputation as a boat eater when a crew from the US Army arrived at the Talkeetna rail station in '58 and began to unload and outfit their bright-yellow vessel. The idea was to chart

As this small plane illustrates, flying in Alaska, whether to enjoy the scenery or to assist in search and rescue, has always been a risky proposition. The plane flipped on an airstrip outside Denali National Park and Preserve in 1930.
DENALI NATIONAL PARK AND PRESERVE MUSEUM COLLECTIONS

the navigable portions of the waterway. Sheldon expressed his skepticism to the lieutenant in charge, according to his biographer. The army scouts were not deterred.

"Lookee," Sheldon told them, "I've got a heck of a lot of fishing traffic up that way in the next few days, and I'll check on your progress from time to time."

And sure enough, when he flew over the canyon two days later, he spotted the wreckage: chunks of the massacred boat floating downstream of the canyon, and the men who'd been aboard perched on a rock ledge next to the surging river. Their circumstances were dire. Without a craft they had no way out of the steep-walled chasm. The current in that stretch of the Big Su, Sheldon said, "is so swift and heavy that even the salmon get beat to death trying to swim upriver."

The pilot had no choice but to attempt rescue. He threaded his plane, a "portly Aeronca Sedan," between the narrowing walls of the canyon, where the turbulence in the air was as dangerous as the waves on the water. He set her down on the roiling river upstream of the stranded scouts, and found himself piloting a craft that no longer responded to his controls. Without airflow over the wings, and on floats that couldn't be steered like wheels or skis, the plane "became an unresponsive deathtrap as it almost immediately began to accelerate downriver with the current."

The plane bucked backward through "combers," careening down the canyon, and Sheldon prayed the engine would stay lit despite the soaking. He floated past the stranded scouts, then accelerated "full throttle" back to them, and managed to get close enough to the ledge for one of the soldiers to clamber onto a float, and into the plane. Then he let the plane ride the rapids backward into smoother water—"one of the longest rides on a river that I've ever taken. It was a shocker." On the downside of the flume, the pilot was able to spin the plane around, take off, and transport his passenger to safety.

And then he turned around and did it again. And again. And again. His final foray on that rescue mission involved rescuing a scout who'd somehow survived the cold, roiling waters and floated far downstream. He was so frozen, Sheldon observed, that he could barely pull himself aboard the aircraft.

Sheldon's achievements in this rescue and others earned him solid and well-deserved respect, but other pilots were equally talented, if arguably less well known. Cliff Hudson was another Talkeetna legend, but one who flew under the radar, in Denali ranger Roger Robinson's estimation. Much of Hudson's aviation rescue work took place on the mountain, and he became one of the park's go-to pilots for SAR missions.

Cliff Hudson arrived in Alaska in 1948 to join his brother's air service business; when Glenn Hudson died in a crash in 1952, Cliff took over. Over the next half a century, he quietly and efficiently transported aspiring

When famed Denali flyer Don Sheldon wasn't aloft on rescues, he provided air taxi services to climbers, flightseers, and photographers, like the one who snapped this picture of the Muldrow Glacier from the window of Sheldon's aircraft.
DENALI NATIONAL PARK AND PRESERVE MUSEUM COLLECTIONS. PHOTO: PETER SANCHEZ

summiters to and from base camps on the High One and neighboring peaks, sometimes in less-than-desirable circumstances.

Tracking down the specifics of rescues Hudson took part in isn't easy; he wasn't interested in fanfare. But one story rises out of the ether, perhaps because it's hitched to the spotlight that shines on Don Sheldon. The two collaborated in the rescue of the survivors of a C-47 that disintegrated in a storm between Anchorage and Fairbanks, leaving wreckage and passengers scattered on Kesugi Ridge in what is now Denali State Park. Ten men died in the accident but six survived, and Hudson was key to bringing the living home.

THE SPOT DEVICE

My whole life has been going into the wilderness without a device.
—DENALI MOUNTAINEERING RANGER ROGER ROBINSON

Personal locator beacons (SPOT, InReach, and others) are demonstrated lifesavers. They provide a level of comfort. They are connection where there would otherwise be no connection. They seem like a foolproof way to stay alive when things go wrong in the backcountry, but you'd be a fool to rely on one.

On a ten-day kayak trip in the Misty Fjords National Monument—Yosemite dropped in the sea, with the nearest civilization a four-hour boat ride away in Ketchikan—one of my partners carried a SPOT device. It had two settings and we only used one: When we arrived safely in our overnight camps, Paula hit the "OK" button, assuring the "real world" we hadn't been swamped by high seas or consumed by a brown bear.

The other was the "Get Me Out of Here Now" button, which would have summoned help if we'd needed it. We never came close to using it. We were blessed with good weather, calm waters, competent navigation, ample food and water, sure feet and hands, and a dearth of bear sightings (though we did hear a bark at one lunch stop, which prompted a quick pack and launch). Fear for life or limb never whispered in our ears or crept up the back of our necks.

If circumstances had twisted, I would have been the likeliest victim. My companions were all Alaskans, experienced kayakers and fluent backwoods travelers in a big, unforgiving country. I am from California, and while I have years of experience as a backpacker, hiker, and skier, in reality I've seldom been more than a few days' walk from a coffee shop. Worse, I was not completely engaged: My husband had informed me mere hours before I boarded the plane to Ketchikan that he wanted a divorce (his timing was abysmal, but that, too, worked out in the end).

What was I thinking as we passed the Eddystone, gateway to the Misty? It struck me there that, regardless of the SPOT device, and the rifle, and the bear spray, I was on my own. My companions didn't know my state of mind and only one would find out during the trip (my tent mate, boat mate, and one of the best people I've had the luck to call a friend). They didn't have to. I had to get along on my own, which meant I'd have to be safe when alone, as well as work effectively with my mates to ensure our safety when we were together.

Or I'd die. SPOT device notwithstanding, rescue was not an option. It was up to me.

My attitude toward backcountry travel—typical for my generation—is no longer the norm, according to every single one of the search-and-rescue veterans I interviewed to compile these stories. To a person, everyone decried the fact that phones and beacons hitched to satellites have, in their experience, become crutches for many who now venture into the backcountry. Levels of preparedness for any contingency, both mental and physical, have sloughed off. The most telling story I heard about how adventurers view technology in the field: Another long-distance kayaker who, when asked about the scariest moment on her long journey, responded it was when her GPS batteries died. Now, says one National Park Service ranger, instead of qualifying with common sense, boots on the ground, and map and compass in hand, people rely on the gadget. In his experience, even a one-page trip plan left with a loved one at home is more effective than technology should you, for whatever reason, get lost in the woods or on the tundra. First, it gives SAR teams a starting point. Second, it demonstrates that you have done your homework, and not just picked up your phone and headed out.

These days, I'm a hybrid. My work as a guidebook writer requires technology; the maps for guides are generated using GPS tracks and waypoints, and my smartphone is always in my pocket. Well, most of the time. I am notorious for forgetting it, or forgetting to charge it, or just plain not answering it.

But my pack is loaded with old-school essentials: map and compass, extra layers, first-aid kit, knife and shovel, emergency blanket. I have my whistle. I tell family and friends where I'm bound, and when I expect to return. If I'm destined to perish in the woods, it won't be because my battery died. And it's likely that I'll be found regardless, even if all that remains are my desiccated bones.

Airborne within an hour of the accident, Hudson pinpointed the location of the survivors before the storm quashed further rescue efforts. The next morning, the weather having sufficiently cleared, Hudson and Sheldon flew to the crash site and found three men stranded in the snow. Sheldon deposited Hudson, equipped with snowshoes and a hatchet, close to the victims and flew off for reinforcements. Hudson, meantime, approached the men and said, "It looks like you boys could use some help." He built a fire to warm them up, and later guided them to where the plane would pick them up. Once the first three were airlifted to safety, Hudson remained in the bush to guide a second wave of rescuers to the wreckage and the remaining three survivors. He received an Air Force commendation for his efforts and then, being a "quiet man," retreated from the limelight, "sort of like the Lone Ranger, doing a good deed and then riding off," according to one of the men he helped rescue.

Upon Hudson's death in 2010, his family noted he'd never wrecked a plane. "Don Sheldon put himself in view," Robinson says, "but the real hero was Cliff Hudson."

For all their successes, flying mountain rescue and air taxis on Denali and other peaks in the Alaska Range was ruthlessly dangerous for flyers. When they crashed, SAR was most often search and recovery, not rescue. The names and stories of colleagues who lost their lives while flying in the park linger in the memories of the park's mountaineering rangers.

Pilot Don Bowers, ranger Cale Schaffer, and volunteer patrol rangers Brian Reagan and Adam Kolff are among those not forgotten. Bowers and Schaffer were both veterans of search-and-rescue operations in Denali National Park and elsewhere; Schaffer worked preventative search and rescue (PSAR) in Grand Canyon National Park before heading to Alaska; Bowers was a veteran of the Iditarod sled-dog race, and had flown a number of SAR missions in the Alaska Range.

A conservative and experienced pilot, Bowers was attempting a landing on the Kahiltna Glacier in June 2000, intending to drop the rangers in relief of a patrol crew coming off the mountain. But the weather was extraordinarily unpredictable. As he approached, conditions abruptly went from flyable to unflyable, and he began to scan the skies for an escape route. The backdoor had closed, he couldn't head out the way he'd come in. He saw daylight, however, to the west, over the Yentna and Lacuna Glaciers, so he flew toward the break in the clouds.

What happened next no one knows for certain. But extraordinarily strong thunderstorms were building around the peak, and Lisa Roderick, who has run Denali's base camp on the Kahiltna for nearly two decades, got word that one of those storms was breaking where Bowers was headed.

His last transmission stated he was returning to base in Talkeetna. Bowers wasn't heard from again. No emergency locator transmitter signal was received. None of the men came back to the little town on the Big Su.

The weather cleared the next day. A multiagency search was launched— air taxis from Talkeetna, fellow rangers on board, and a C-130 from the military. It took eight hours to locate the plane, which had crashed at the toe of the Yentna Glacier. The wings of the Cessna 185 had come off in flight and were found some distance from the fuselage, testament to the down shear forces at play in the storm. All four men were lost.

One of the most remarkable search and recovery efforts in Denali National Park occurred decades before the Kahiltna became a landing strip for air taxis and a base camp for mountaineering and scientific expeditions. In 1944 an army C-47 from Elmendorf Air Force Base in Anchorage disappeared in the Alaska Range east of Denali. After several days of searching, the wreckage was discovered; the aircraft had collided with a twelve-thousand-foot-high peak now known as Mount Deception. All nineteen men aboard perished.

The exact circumstances of the crash will never be known. In those days navigation relied on map and compass; this worked well when the weather was clear, but clear weather can't be relied on in the Alaska Range. Another confounding factor: Altimeters could be off by as much as a thousand feet due to pressure changes. Modern pilots and those familiar with the erratic air generated by Denali and the surrounding peaks speculate the pilot of the ill-fated airship never saw the mountain. Mount McKinley National Park's acting superintendent, Grant Pearson, having been persuaded to assist in the recovery, notes that as the plane he was aboard neared the glacier where the wreckage had been sighted, "the bomber hit a sudden down draft. We lost a thousand feet before we could level off. 'That,' I said, when my teeth had stopped rattling, 'is probably what happened to that other plane.'"

When a military plane goes down, its personnel are considered missing in action. The MIA designation put the army in charge of collection of evidence, and the crash site on Mount Deception was declared off-limits until the recovery was complete. Once the C-47's wreckage was located, despite its remoteness and Pearson's reticence—he, like so many involved in SAR, worried about placing living men in danger to retrieve the dead—a major recovery mission was launched. Forty-four men, including the superintendent, trekked through then-unmapped regions of the park, most of them inexperienced and unprepared for the challenges of such an undertaking.

Despite his reluctance and the hardships posed by having to teach the men he was working with everything from how to use crampons to how to avoid frostbite, Pearson found himself part of a well-outfitted operation. Sled-dog teams were replaced with "snorting" M-7 snow tractors, said to be able to go anywhere a dog could, but capable of hauling more equipment. A "radio-truck-trailer" with the capacity to send messages worldwide was stationed at Wonder Lake, and the recovery team equipped with twenty-six-pound radios. "We had two army trucks full of ropes, tents, stoves, food, ice axes, crampons, and other climbing accouterments," Pearson recalled. "We had two snow tractors, two wounded personnel trailers, one caterpillar bulldozer plus an airplane to drop supplies when we got higher up. It was the most thoroughly motorized mountain-climbing expedition in history."

He also enlisted the help of photographer and alpinist Bradford Washburn, whose iconic images of Denali earned him a significant place in mountaineering history; he was the man who, shooting from an aircraft, scouted the West Buttress route that most climbers use to ascend to the summit to this day.

Over the next six weeks, Pearson and his expedition made their way up glaciers and over mountain passes to the crash site, where they set up a final camp and did what they could to locate the missing men. Digging through the wreckage, however, they found only bloodstains. Washburn and a few companions climbed to an engine higher on the glacier; no one was found there either, but the men decided to tag the top of the peak while they were so close.

In the end, as winter's freeze began to settle onto Denali's high country, Pearson decided to retreat. The powers-that-were at Elmendorf agreed with his decision, and the superintendent was awarded a Congressional Medal of Freedom for his efforts.

As for the C-47 and its crew, they have rested in stillness on the ice for the better part of a century. Pearson's thoughts on that remotest of graveyards is poignant, and perhaps others who've lost loved ones in Alaska's unmapped places can find comfort in his words. "What finer resting place could they have," the ranger wrote, "cradled in that beautiful, rugged, virgin country, deep under a perpetual blanket of clean white snow, guarded by northern lights in winter and the midnight sun in summer?"

Ptarmigan Peak

The steep peaks of the Chugach Range are Anchorage's stunning backdrop and backyard playground. Pleated with chutes and couloirs—narrow corridors where snow accumulates between rock faces—the Chugach tower over Turnagain Arm. When the weather cooperates, particularly in late spring and early summer, these white lines, streaking from ridgetops to the sea, entice ice climbers and skiers from the nearby city and beyond.

Snow is meant to slide in chutes, especially when a certain set of conditions are met. Prime avalanche conditions require a slope angled at between thirty and forty-five degrees. One of the snowfall depositions must be unstable—ball bearings or sugar or ice—something the next layer of snow can slip on. The trigger can be an earthquake, another deposit of snow, the warmth of the spring sun, the edge of a ski. Then the mountains shuck their loads down these perpetually open paths.

When these conditions aren't present, the chutes and couloirs of the Chugach are quiescent. That's when humans attempt something unnatural. They climb up what's designed for things to go down. They head in through the out door. They defy gravity with ice axes and crampons. But that doesn't mean the mountains won't shuck them off anyway.

By all accounts, the fourteen people who ascended the two-thousand-foot North Couloir of Ptarmigan Peak, a 4,839-foot summit not far southeast of Anchorage, enjoyed their ascent. The weather conditions on June 28, 1997, were comfortable: sunshine, warmth, a little wind. The climbers, ranging in age from teenagers to a couple of women in their early forties, were part of a wilderness studies class at the University of Alaska

Anchorage (UAA). For weeks they'd been studying mountaineering techniques and practicing skills under the tutelage of a pair of experienced alpinists and instructors. They'd been taught how to use their ice axes and crampons, how to set anchors, tie knots, and work ropes. They gelled as a team, aware of each other's weaknesses and strengths. The foundation was solid, and it was time to begin building on it in the real world.

In hindsight, given the relative inexperience of the students, it's not surprising the ascent took a little longer than expected. Also not surprising: When classmates and instructors attained the summit ridge they lingered there, taking in the views and savoring the accomplishment. All this, again, took a little longer than expected.

It was late in the long day when they began their descent—about 5 p.m., the time they'd planned to complete the climb. They had a lot of daylight left, and they had a choice. They could descend the walk-off route, a longer, safer trail down the south side of the peak, or they could head back the way they'd come. Given the hour, they chose the shorter route, exiting via the same couloir they'd climbed. They'd come in the out door; they'd go out that way too.

This was the first of several decisions that would later be analyzed, criticized, and agonized over, which is only natural given the terrifying chain of events that followed. Daryl Miller, the veteran mountaineering ranger who spent much of his career in Denali, contemplates Ptarmigan Peak with concern and dismay even decades later. How could he not, given the scale of the accident, the losses involved, and his own place in the story. Hindsight is a bible, imparting new insights with each review.

After choosing the couloir as their exit route, the class roped up in four teams, with three or four people on each rope, separated by fifteen to twenty feet. Instructor Ben Greene was part of the first team of four; instructor Deb Greene was with the third team, also of four. The second and fourth teams were composed of three students each. The idea was to "plunge step" down the snowfield, the climbers kicking the heels of their boots into the snow with force, creating a platform underfoot. Given conditions in the couloir late on that lovely summer day, plunge stepping seemed a reasonable option.

The chutes and couloirs of the Chugach are reflected in the still waters of Turnagain Arm.
PHOTO: TRACY SALCEDO

But as Miller and other alpinists know well, soft ice makes it easier for ice axes to slide free and for climbers to lose purchase. By the time the class began its descent, things were getting mushy. The instructors noticed their students slipping and having difficulty self-arresting, a combination of lack of experience and inadequate equipment. As they reached steeper terrain, members of each team belayed each other: While one climber was moving, the other climbers thrust the shafts of their ice axes into the snow, human anchors in the event the climber on the move slid out. Another red flag in hindsight: The only way a rope can, with any surety, stop a fall is if it is secured to rock or ice. If it's connected only to another climber, the forces that come into play when a human being peels loose are virtually impossible for another human being to arrest. Ropes without bomber anchors, especially in soft, slick snow, provide only the illusion of security, as insubstantial as air.

When climber Jacob Franck, on the highest rope team and alongside teammate Eric Schlemme, lost his footing and began to slide, the domino effect came into play. The other climbers on his rope braced themselves, with no effect. Though they held fast to their ice axes with their toes dug in, the downward force applied to the harnesses at their waists transformed their feet into fulcrums. One by one they pinged free onto their backs with their ice axes in hand, and started to slide.

Now another confounding factor came into play: the format of the descent. The instructors had set up a "horizontal system," with each team moving in a line, one above the other, separated by fifteen to thirty feet. Like a bowling ball in a stone alley, the first team rocketed down the lane and collided with the team below. Only the pins couldn't scatter because they were roped together. Instead they converged, became bound even more tightly in the tumbling, ice axes in hand but disconnected from the mountain. The mass of seven slammed into the next team down, with the same result. The fourth team heard the knot of falling bodies, tangled ropes, and sharp gear coming, but there was nothing they could do. They braced. They were hit. They became part of the disaster.

The class ended up in a bloody snarl of ropes and bodies in the boulder field at the base of the couloir. People were suffocating in the mash-up, unable to free themselves or each other. Two of the climbers, twenty-three-year-old Steven Brown and forty-year-old Mary Ellen Fogarty, perished in the long slide. The rest were injured to varying degrees, suffering broken bones, lacerations, punctures, and blunt-force trauma.

What transpired next wasn't so much search and rescue as just rescue. A trio of skiers who had witnessed the accident rushed to the scene and began cutting the ropes and moving the victims away from each other so they could breathe. Mountain bikers on a nearby trail also saw the accident and came to the climbers' aid, one calling 911 while the others were recruited by the skiers to help. The bikers and skiers wrapped the survivors in sleeping bags, space blankets, and as much comfort as they could muster among the boulders at the foot of the mountain.

Dr. Ken Zafren, medical director for the Alaska Mountain Rescue Group (AMRG) and an emergency physician based in Anchorage, was airlifted to the site and one of the first to arrive. He called the sight "surreal," with skiers, mountain bikers, and now rescuers, some in shorts and T-shirts, doing their best to unravel and triage the injured and dead.

Zafren and the others were joined in short order by reinforcements from AMRG, as well as rescue teams from Chugach State Park, Alaska State Troopers (AST), the Anchorage fire and police departments, and the Alaska Air National Guard's 210th Pararescue Squadron. More aircraft were brought online, with an AST helicopter carrying rescuers from AMRG, a pair of Pave Hawk helicopters dropping nine parajumpers and their medical supplies. Zafren and Master Sergeant Brent Woodiness triaged the patients, coordinated their airlifts and, over the next several hours, the Pave Hawks transported the injured from couloir to emergency room. An Air National Guard C-130 circled overhead, refueling the copters so they could work steadily over the four hours it took to get all the victims off the mountain. In all, ninety-three rescuers, including the skiers and cyclists first to the scene, came to the climbers' aid.

The story of Ptarmigan Peak doesn't end with the rescue. What happens in the field is only one aspect of the work. Preparation is another; analysis is a third. Looking back and figuring out what happened—and how it could be avoided in the future—is where Miller stepped in.

"How could it happen? A mess like that?" he wanted to know and so did the University of Alaska.

The school asked *American Alpine Journal* editor Jed Williamson to conduct an independent review of the accident. To find out more, Williamson, Miller, and Jim Ratz, past director for the National Outdoor Leadership School (NOLS), climbed the Ptarmigan couloir to see for themselves what the class had attempted and encountered in the chute. They interviewed the instructors, the students, their families, and officials at UAA, exploring not only the mechanics of the accident itself, but also the mentalities of the climbers and teachers, and the academic foundations of the wilderness studies course. After exhaustive review, Miller and his cohorts found they could place blame—or perhaps better, responsibility—on all players. They found fault in the instructors' decision not to fix anchors on the slope or create a bomber multi-anchor belay; in the students' inexperience; in the instructors' choice to stack teams horizontally; in the students' reticence to say "no" because of ignorance and/or peer pressure; in the high ratio of students to instructors; in the route choice based on a variety of factors, including the boulder field at the end of the run-out; in the university's assumption that just because the Ptarmigan couloir had been safe for wilderness education to date translated to continued safety. All of these things and more were analyzed and criticized. In the end, the investigators asserted, "The safest alternative would have been to descend via the walk-off route."

The report didn't please anyone—not the families of the students injured and killed, the instructors, or the university, though the school did take a hard look at its wilderness studies curriculum and make significant changes based on the critical recommendations. But assigning blame—and by extension, releasing others from blame—wasn't the point. Targeting the failures that led to the incident, whatever their genesis, was both applicable and instructive for future climbers on Ptarmigan and elsewhere. The red flags were flying but were ignored or not recognized. With the failings called out, perhaps students with misgivings would feel more comfortable speaking up and not giving in to peer pressure. Mountaineering instructors would better understand the limitations of and risks posed by the skill levels of members of their classes, and by sun-softened snow, and by the belay systems they choose. The assumptions of the university about route choice were blown apart—the idea that it was OK to climb a north-facing couloir that held snow all summer because that's what had been done in past years, without incident, was completely debunked. The report upended the culture in the UAA's wilderness education program from top to bottom.

One veteran alpinist makes an interesting observation about how Alaska's mountaineering culture, writ large, may have played into the events on Ptarmigan Peak. When he saw the couloir in the aftermath, he was astounded. He's a climber, too, a longtime friend of Miller's, and they've shared high adventure together a number of times in a number of wilder-nesses. He's based in Colorado, however, where the mountains are, argu-ably, kinder and gentler.

"I might have taken a look at that thing and said, 'We don't climb those in Colorado,'" he observed. "And someone might have said, 'This is Alaska, man. We do these things. You gotta get your head right.'"

What the Ptarmigan events highlight, Miller and others have noted, is that disasters are cumulative. You can make a mistake in the backcountry—even a big one, like crashing your airplane in a winter storm—and still make it out alive if the decisions you make after that crash (provided you survive) are good ones. On Ptarmigan Peak, sketchy decisions that, taken individually, might not have had dire consequences became deadly when compounded. Good decisions made by search-and-rescue teams, coupled with experience and luck, turned the tide for the North Couloir survivors. The efficacy of the rescue was never called into question. In the jumble of boulders at the base of Ptarmigan Peak, the fallen were unraveled, triaged, and transferred to hospital with all good speed and professionalism.

In the glaring light of hindsight, the tangle of Ptarmigan holds many les-sons. Don't be lulled by good weather; sunshine, like storm, may also con-jure challenge and danger. Use secure anchors. Climb within your physical and mental limits. Don't let your guard down on the descent: It's the gnar-liest part of any climb. If you make a mistake, do your best to rectify it. And study up: You can learn from the mistakes of others.

"Whose Son Do You Want Me to Send?"

———

S AR. Search and rescue. Search and recovery. Search and reconciliation. Not search and remorse.

Whenever possible, the remains of those who've lost their lives in Alaska's backcountry are retrieved and returned to family. But sometimes they remain where they lie. The matrix changes if the subject of a search is either known to have expired or if the likelihood of survival is nil. In those circumstances, Denali mountaineering ranger Mark Westman explains, rescuers consider two key questions: Is it worth it? Is the risk too great?

The decision is never simple. The factors at play within the SAR operation are changeable, subject to interpretation, muddled by emotion. *The weather has lifted; we can fly now. Those hikers carried adequate fuel and food; they could be holed up in a snow cave somewhere; we can find them. I know those climbers; they have excellent skills and endurance; they could still be alive.*

Another powerful driver in making the recovery call is the emotional cost to the living. When the fallen is a comrade, and particularly if the remains have been traumatized, incident commanders must consider who should be sent on the mission. It's difficult enough to reclaim an anonymous body from a mountainside or the deep woods, because even if you don't know the person, someone does—and that person is grieving. When the body belongs to someone you know personally or work with, the potential for long-lasting emotional trauma is amped up.

Some things, rescuers say, you just can't un-see. Denali's Daryl Miller recalled a plane crash on the mountain; the airship came apart in flight. The bodies of those who perished in the accident were badly burned. One of those killed was a colleague. Miller's experience in Vietnam, where he'd

The sun silhouettes the wilderness of Denali.
PHOTO: TRACY SALCEDO

witnessed firsthand the carnage of war, prompted him to deny permission for the rangers under his command to remove the remains of the crash victims. At least one of those rangers was angry. But Miller knew that the individual, and any other rescuers with ties to the victims, would be better off mad in the short term than emotionally scarred for the long run.

"You don't get used to them," Miller said, reflecting on recovering bodies. "You never get used to them."

Outside forces also come to bear. Sometimes the families of those lost in the wild push hard for more effort, more time. Sometimes they say *don't bother*.

The stories of climbers in trouble on Mount Johnson, of a midnight rescue, and of the loss of two treasured alpinists on Mount Foraker, illuminate the rescuers' dilemma.

ICEFALL

The summit of Mount Johnson, a coveted spire overlooking Denali's massive Ruth Glacier, was the goal of climbers Seth Shaw and Tom Wagner. The two men were flown onto the river of ice in May 2000 to make their attempt on the peak, and successfully completed the climb on May 21. They retreated to their base camp, where they then spent the better part of a week pinned down by inclement weather.

When conditions improved, the mountaineers decided to attempt another climb. They skied to the base of an icefall with an overhanging serac; a giant block of ice that created a cave at the base. Wagner went inside the cave, under the block, to scope a route while Shaw remained on the slope outside, intending to snap a photo. The overhanging serac collapsed on them both.

It took Wagner thirty minutes to dig himself out from under a boulder of ice. When he was finally free and able to search for his partner, he could find no trace. The place he'd last seen Shaw was buried under ice boulders twenty to thirty feet deep. And the ice kept coming.

The injured Wagner—he suffered a broken leg—retreated to the camp of another party of climbers on the Ruth, setting search and rescue for Shaw in motion. One of those climbers skied to Mountain House, located in the amphitheater above the storied Ruth Gorge, where he hoped to radio for help. Meanwhile, three other climbers headed back to the accident site to see if they could locate the missing mountaineer. They found nothing but gear: skis, a backpack, ice axes that appeared to have been blown down from the site by the blast force of the icefall.

The day after the accident, a Talkeetna Air Taxi pilot was able to pick up the injured Wagner and transport him to the hospital. The park service's high-altitude Lama helicopter flew to the site carrying mountaineering rangers Roger Robinson and Steve Metcalf, who scoured the debris field shooting video and looking for sign of the missing man. But in the end, searches both by air and on the ground were halted. The site was just too remote, the hazards too great. Rangers involved in the search and rescue noted seracs commonly calved from the glacier in that area, and even as the search for Shaw was underway, the accident site was pummeled by frozen debris.

But questions remain. As the *American Alpine Journal* notes, no one knows why Shaw and Wagner ventured into the "precarious area" in the first place, given the dangers that, in the end, prevented rescuers from effecting a ground search for the missing man. And Shaw's final resting place has yet to be discovered. The unknowns are powerful enough to remain foremost in rescuers' minds even as the years pass.

"RANGER! RANGER!"

It's the middle of the night at seventeen thousand feet. The temperature is twenty degrees below zero, the wind is blowing forty miles per hour. And someone rushes up to your tent screaming, "Ranger! Ranger!"

It's not the kind of wake-up call anyone wants to get.

It's also something that can only happen if you are a mountaineering ranger at high camp on North America's tallest mountain.

On this night, Mark Westman found himself facing hard choices. The report was of a climber in trouble on what's known as the Autobahn, a glacial slope below Denali Pass with a reputation. Take a slide on the Autobahn and you pick up speed quickly; pick up speed quickly on Denali, and you might not stop for thousands of feet.

The climber in distress was suffering from high-altitude pulmonary edema (HAPE) and hypothermia. Either condition can be life threatening; in combination, the odds of survival are just plain awful. But both can be treated: For HAPE the cure is to lose altitude as quickly as possible; for hypothermia the cure is to warm the victim as quickly as possible. Neither was going to be an easy task on this night, in these conditions.

"The crux for me," Westman recalls, "was do we do it? We aren't required to go. He was far enough away to be a pain, but close enough for us to think we could do this and do it without putting ourselves in danger."

Westman decided to try. He and Denali's other rangers had trained for this scenario, though they'd not yet had to execute it in real life: "We'd hoped it would never happen." Now it had, and this was not the "light" version. Denali was raging, and the rescuers would have to bring the freezing man down off the Autobahn via a steep side-hill traverse.

The ranger rounded up four volunteers and five guides in the high camp; the ten rescuers then ventured together into the night. Westman's priority was to keep his companions warm: Denali was not only conjuring bone-chilling wind, but now snow was falling hard as well. "Nobody dies, nobody comes back with frostbite," Westman vowed. "I'm not going to get anyone hurt for this." In his mind a mental bumper sticker: *Your emergency is not my emergency.*

When the midnight search-and-rescue team reached the victim, the man looked right at them, took off his jacket, and threw it into the wind. It sounds counterintuitive, but "paradoxical undressing" is not uncommon in what's called lethal hypothermia—the final stages of freezing to death. As the body's temperature drops below ninety degrees Fahrenheit, all systems begin to fail. Blood vessels that constricted earlier in the process suddenly dilate, shunting the blood that had been protecting the body's core back to the surface and extremities, a sudden flood of circulation that makes the victim feel overheated. Finding people dead of exposure but stripped to their underwear is not out of the ordinary.

Westman and his partners knew the climber's window of survival was slipping away, but they weren't about to give up on him. Over the next six to seven hours, yelling directions to each other over the wind because they were in a radio dead zone, they rigged rope systems to span crevasses and inched the victim toward high camp.

Despite their efforts, the afflicted mountaineer passed away about twenty minutes before the rescuers reached the safety of the tent. With the wind chill, Westman figured the temperature was fifty to sixty degrees below zero; even if they had gotten him to shelter sooner, the ranger isn't sure the victim would have lived. But the rescuers had done their job, had done their best, and hadn't suffered a casualty on the team, of any kind. The dilemma had been considered, and while the outcome was far from satisfactory, the risk had been successfully calculated.

THE MATRIX OF SURVIVABILITY

For all that each search and rescue depends on the personal decisions, experience, and characters of the SAR team members, rescuers also employ an objective matrix—a "survivability analysis"—to determine when and if a search should be initiated, or called off. The analysis takes into consideration the objective elements—both natural and man-made—that determine whether a lost climber might still be alive on a mountain, or a kayaker in a river gorge, or a hunter in the woods. How much fuel was the person carrying? How has the weather behaved since the disappearance? How high are the winds? How many days overdue is the person? The elements are scored, the decision is made, and it holds, even as emotion washes in.

The first time the survivability analysis was applied in Denali National Park and Preserve was when climbers Karen McNeill and Sue Nott disappeared on 17,355-foot Mount Foraker, the second highest peak in the Alaska Range. The two first-class mountaineers were taking on the challenge of the *Infinite Spur*, considered one of the most difficult alpine routes in North America. Despite the *Spur's* cachet, Nott and McNeill, who had tackled the challenging Cassin Ridge on Denali in 2004, wouldn't have the same possibility of finding help or soliciting the support of other teams if they encountered trouble—something they'd had on the High One. Foraker, also called Denali's Wife, is less traveled, less accessible, and less forgiving.

But McNeill and Nott had the skills and experience to make it there and back again safely, whether or not they claimed the summit in the process. They departed base camp on the Kahiltna Glacier on May 12, 2006, outfitted with a radio, food for fourteen days, and enough fuel to melt water for approximately twenty days. They used skis to make the approach, which they stashed, along with a small cache of food and fuel for the final leg of the return, on a pass between the Kahiltna base camp and the foot of the spur. They met another pair of climbers on the approach on May 14. That was the last time they were seen.

The only thing that can be confirmed about what transpired in those days between last contact and the start of the search-and-rescue operation is bad weather. Planes were grounded intermittently throughout the period, so getting aloft to check the climbers' progress was impossible. Then a windstorm such as only the Alaska Range can generate settled over both Foraker and Denali, generating gusts exceeding one hundred miles per hour, strong enough to blow alpinists clear off a slope. Dubbed a "wind event," conditions pinned climbers down on both mountains. No one was going anywhere.

The winds died in the final days of the month. By that time the fourteen-day window within which Nott and McNeill were expected to return had closed. No word. Pilots from Talkeetna scanned the route and the approach whenever Foraker permitted. No sightings. Tracks leading to the base of the route were discovered, but nothing appeared above. No signs of life.

On June 1 Daryl Miller, then chief ranger acting out of the Talkeetna district, initiated the formal search and rescue. On and off for the next ten days, as conditions permitted, the park's high-altitude Lama helicopter and fixed-wing aircraft flew multiple passes over the route, its approaches, and its exits, logging twenty-seven flight hours, with rangers taking hundreds of photographs. A day into the search Nott's backpack was discovered in a debris cone at the base of the spur. The radio was inside, as was her sleeping bag; a fleece jacket was found nearby. Later a fleece cap was recovered, a yellow stuff sack, a pink shell jacket. Higher up, tracks led to a high point at 16,600 feet, near the mountain's false summit. At that point, say those in the know, McNeill and Nott could no longer retreat down the *Infinite Spur*. At that point they became summiters; they had to go over the top to get back down.

Then the weather closed in again, and rescuers were forced to stand down. By the time conditions permitted renewal of the SAR operation, twenty-eight days had passed since Nott and McNeill were last seen. Members of their families had congregated in Talkeetna, waiting, hoping. The mountaineering community was doing the same, both on the slopes of Denali and farther afield. Beloved, competent, experienced, intelligent, strong: It was inconceivable—next to impossible—to think Karen McNeill and Sue Nott were lost forever … to let them go.

But that's what Miller and the others had to do. The survivability analysis took place. Fuel, temperature, wind, food, days overdue: The score told the story. The search was scaled back on June 11, and formally called off on July 14.

"When you call off a search, it's big," Miller observed as he reflected on the events. He was speaking in generalities, but the *Infinite Spur* was foremost on his mind. "You'd better be able to take the heat. The heat from the family that's in the ranger station asking, why aren't we searching anymore?"

That's when another hard question must be asked, the retired ranger said. "Whose son do you want me to send?"

DENALI

Denali amplifies everything. It catches storms blown in off the Bering Sea and makes them bigger. It conjures its own storms, wrapping slopes and ridges in frigid vortexes and confining expeditions to their tents for days. The mountain's vertical relief—about eighteen thousand feet from base to summit—is greater than that found on Mount Everest in the Himalaya. Denali tests competence and attitude; it magnifies success and failure. It takes skill, will, and luck to stand on the 20,310-foot-high summit. All of North America lies below.

These days, about eleven hundred people attempt to climb the High One each year. For a seasoned mountaineer, an ascent via the West Buttress route—the most commonly climbed on the peak—could be considered a walk-up. A fit person with a good guide and a working knowledge of glacier travel and rope work has as reasonable a chance of reaching Denali's summit via the West Buttress as an experienced alpinist, but only about half make it. Those who don't are usually slapped back by persistent storms or a failure to acclimate to the altitude. They retreat to base camp on the Kahiltna Glacier, catch their flights back to Talkeetna, and their adventures become stories shared with friends and family around kitchen tables and campfires.

The roof of North America has been a mountaineering magnet for more than a century. Denali is one of the Seven Summits, coveted by thousands whose bucket lists include standing on the highest point on each continent. Because of its challenges, Denali is both goal and training ground for those aspiring to the eight-thousand-meter goliaths of the Himalaya and Karakoram. It's not as tall, but Denali's remoteness and northern latitude make it one of the most difficult ascents on the planet.

The history of mountaineering on Denali is short in the grand scheme. The mountain was the stuff of legends among the native Athabascans who roamed its skirts for generations, but there's no evidence they climbed it. There was really no reason to: The resources they relied on to survive and thrive—sheep, caribou, moose, berries—couldn't be found on Denali's ice rivers and stony ridgelines. And for the first European and Russian explorers venturing into what would become known as Alaska, Denali was just a white cloud on the horizon on a clear day, distant and barricaded by rivers swollen with snowmelt, thickets of forest and expanses of tundra, maddening swarms of mosquitoes, and temperatures that froze limbs.

But by the turn of the twentieth century, as competition to conquer all remaining extremes on the planet heated up, the mountain became a prize for gentleman adventurers. Rich, white, and ambitious, alpinists and explorers from the eastern United States and beyond ponied up time and money to take a stab at being the first to the top.

A flurry of activity surrounded Denali's first ascent in 1913. Frauds and sourdoughs and future champions of what would soon become a national park launched expeditions, and Denali denied them all. In the end, a party composed of Harry Karstens, the man who would become the future park's first superintendent; Walter Harper, a native Alaskan; Hudson Stuck, Alaska's archdeacon; and missionary Robert Tatum claimed the summit. What's commonly referred to as the Stuck expedition followed a trail blazed by three-time aspiring summiters Belmore Browne and Professor Herschel Parker. The third Browne expedition was halted by weather within two hundred feet of the summit. On the retreat they camped on the Muldrow Glacier, hoping to rest up and regroup before the long trek back to civilization. Those plans were thwarted with the explosion of Novarupta, the volcano that created the Valley of Ten Thousand Smokes in Katmai National Park and Preserve, more than four hundred miles to the south. The eruption set off avalanches that threatened the team and shattered the summit trail they'd created. The Browne expedition made it out without aid of any kind despite the disaster; the Stuck expedition also descended safely off the peak, despite having to hack its way through jumbled blocks of ice where Browne and crew had climbed a smooth highway before the eruption.

. In fact, every group that made an attempt on the summit in those halcyon days made it out without assistance—even the Sourdoughs, a team comprised of miners from Kantishna who sought to do what the gentleman summiters had thus far failed to accomplish. Though its veracity has been called into question, the story is worth retelling: In 1910 two members of the four-man team reached the summit of Denali's North Peak, about a thousand feet below the 20,310-foot South Peak, and planted a 14-foot-long spruce flagpole they'd dragged up over glacier and crevasse. The idea was that the pole and flag could be seen, on a clear day, from Fairbanks to the north, proving the Sourdoughs, fueled on summit day by doughnuts and coffee, had accomplished what the dandies from Outside could not.

After the summit was claimed and the national park established (peak and park were both dubbed Mount McKinley back in the day), decades passed before anyone tried to reach the top again. That next attempt—the intertwined story of the Lindley-Liek and Cosmic Ray expeditions—was both successful and required search and rescue, and is chronicled in this section. It was the start of a long tradition of exceptional SAR efforts in the park.

DENALI'S RESCUE MOUNTAINEERS

Like everything else, Denali amplifies SAR. The mountaineering rangers who spearhead and execute search and rescue in the park are among the best in the world, and have been working to meet and exceed their own stellar reputations for decades. Starting in the 1980s, as the number of aspiring summiters began to steadily climb, the rangers based out of Talkeetna, located south of both mountain and park at the confluence of the Chulitna, Talkeetna, and Susitna Rivers, began their evolution. It's not only about their technical skills; it's also about their experience. Their dedication to Denali, to those who explore its flanks and seek its summit, and to each other, permeates town and park, and radiates throughout the state.

The impact Denali's mountaineering rangers have on search and rescue throughout Alaska became clear in the first interviews I conducted for this book. I called the Alaska State Troopers; I called various national and state parks; I called volunteer rescue groups. What are the stories you would tell? I asked. They had ideas, but they also said I needed to go to Denali.

This deference to the rangers working on the mountain points up, yet again, that teamwork in search and rescue reaches beyond jurisdiction. Denali's rangers possess expertise in all aspects, from logistics at base camp to operations in extreme weather and at extreme altitudes, making them a go-to resource for neighboring Alaskan parks such as Wrangell-St. Elias, and on peaks in Canada's Yukon Territory and British Columbia. The Alaska State Troopers, military units, the state parks, and the volunteer organizations all understand the capabilities of their counterparts on the mountain. They train together so they can work smoothly together. One example: The air force's parajumpers have trained on the peak for years. In collaboration with the park service the PJs have flown supplies to the medical camp at 14,200 feet, and landed on the "Football Field," about a thousand feet below Denali's airy summit, to assist with rescues. No one agency claims top honors in the field of search and rescue, but those working for the park service in Denali have earned respect of Alaskan proportions for the work they've done over the years, the experience they've accumulated, and their dedication to service.

OLD AND BOLD: THE GRAND MASTERS OF DENALI SAR

Mountaineers who lose their lives on daring adventures or ascents, whether in Yosemite or the Himalaya or Alaska, almost always grab the headlines. As the saying goes, there are old climbers and there are bold climbers, but there are no old, bold climbers.

But this isn't strictly true. Sometimes the bold ones accomplish amazing things that go unheralded, and then simply, quietly, go on doing what they do. They simply, quietly, go on living.

Denali tends to reel in rangers and keep them. The pull of the mountain and the calling can be lifelong. Daryl Miller served as Denali's chief mountaineering ranger from 1991 to 2008; he's now retired and living in Anchorage. Roger Robinson has served on the mountain for decades as well, and while he's no longer on the sharp end of the search-and-rescue rope, he was in the ranger station into 2019, working jobs just as integral to the success of a rescue mission as flying the airships and rigging the belays. As was the case when I asked for Alaskan search-and-rescue stories and was pointed to Denali, when I arrived in Denali and asked who to talk to, I was pointed to Miller and Robinson.

Daryl Miller is a respected member of the growing class of old, bold climbers. When he sat down for an interview in 2018, he possessed an air of wistfulness as he spoke about search and rescue in the Alaska and Chugach Ranges, where he built his career and reputation. I didn't ask about it because it didn't seem like an appropriate question for a stranger to ask: "You seem a little sad. Why?" His reputation as a brilliant tactician and a spark plug preceded him, as did a diagnosis of Parkinson's disease, and even as we sat, he emanated a special kind of energy. If I were incapacitated in a blinding snowstorm at eighteen thousand feet on Denali and this man showed up, trusting him with my life would be a no-brainer.

But now I wonder: Was it the challenges of Parkinson's that tamped him down? Was it a longing to be back on the mountain—any mountain? Perhaps it was just his nature, but what became clear to me after meeting him, talking with his friends and colleagues, and reading about his life, was that Miller, in the face of illness or any other challenge thrown his way, would blaze his own trail.

Miller's exploits as a marine, a chimp wrestler, a rodeo clown, and more are the stuff of another story. His accomplishments as a mountaineer would fill its own volume, and one of the best chapters would be the story of his circumnavigation of Denali in winter with partner Mark Stasik in 1995. Circumnavigation of the mountain had been done before, by Dr. Frederick Cook, whose goal was actually to be the first man on the mountain's summit (he failed badly on that score, perpetrating a legendary fraud in the process). For Cook, the circumnavigation was a sorry second. Miller and Stasik, however, took on the challenge intentionally. Pictures on a wall in the Talkeetna ranger station document the epic adventure—the snow pigs (their sleds), the cold, the dark, the broken ski and snowshoes, the 350 miles of trail breaking, route finding, river crossing, crevasse negotiating, pass climbing. The subtitle: "Cold, wet, tired and hungry—and then your tent catches on fire."

Sound like the stuff of a rescue? Not for Miller. Part of what kept him alive, whether he was involved in a SAR on Denali or climbing somewhere in the Alaska Range for fun, was the assumption that no one was ever going to help him out. These days, taking on a challenge like a circumnavigation of the Denali-Foraker massif is an entirely different animal. Improved technology and the reduced sense of personal responsibility it confers has become a pervasive mindset for backcountry travelers. "I feel people depend too much on the park service or other things to get them out if they get in trouble," Miller says.

Miller's long career on Denali delivered some of the best and worst moments of his life. Topping the list of bests: adventure and camaraderie. Over long days in the backcountry with friends and colleagues, Miller and his cohort became familiar with Denali park's six million acres in the same way their storied predecessors, Harry Karstens and Grant Pearson, had decades before. They tramped the tundra, the ridgelines, the glaciers, the braided river valleys, the hollows and high points, and came to understand the risks that Denali imposes without prejudice.

Given his calling, it seemed logical to ask if Miller had ever been the subject of a search and rescue himself. He was quick to shake his head no. It would be impossible, he said, to live such a request down. He recalled a traverse he'd made with partner Keith Nicholson following Ohio Creek to park headquarters. Five feet of snow fell in twenty-four hours, which made traveling impossible and forced them into the Bull River, which was not frozen. They spent the next three days in and out of the water as they covered seventeen miles to safety.

"Nicholson wanted a rescue; I said no way," Miller recalled. "We still had bagels, we had tea. We were OK. Where I work, Daryl being rescued? They'd never let me live that down."

———

Sitting across the conference table in the Talkeetna ranger station, ranger Roger Robinson does an excellent job of deflecting. As we talk about different rescues on the mountain, he doesn't speak much about the role he has played in many of them—a reticence that's common among rescuers.

Instead, he focuses on another passion—aeronautics. Robinson has closely followed the evolution of the use of airships for rescue on the mountain. When, for example, he relates the story of a rescue involving Ray Genet, a legendary climber and guide on Denali, and one of the three men who claimed the peak's epic first winter ascent, the emphasis is as much on the helicopter and its pilot as it is on any other aspect of the mission, or on the mountaineering.

And it's a good story. In 1976 an all women's team had reached Denali's summit via the South Buttress and was on the descent when a pair of the climbers slipped, fell, suffered injuries, and were forced to bivouac at nineteen thousand feet. Aviator Buddy Woods was enlisted in the ensuing rescue, and Genet, who was acclimatized to the altitude, also signed up for the mission.

"Buddy had a small helicopter with a jet engine in it," Robinson explained. It had a lot of power but was untested: These were "early times for that type of ship." Woods deposited a stash of fuel at sixteen thousand feet on the buttress, then flew back down the mountain, stripped the copter of its battery, and loaded up Genet. The ship landed on the summit and off-loaded the guide—"Ray got out and took a picture"—and then Genet descended to the assistance of the climbers.

"Ray got them up and walking down; he made them walk," Robinson said with a smile, then added that Woods returned to pick them up farther down the mountain. The flight, and the rescue, amounted to "unbelievable drama."

Robinson, an Oregon native, first started climbing in Alaska in 1975, and by 1980 had basically parked himself in Denali, having spent a hundred days climbing in the range. The park brought him on board, and he's been a fixture ever since. He and Miller first met in 1986, but the two wouldn't start working together until 1989, when Robinson invited Miller, who was living in a teepee at the time, to apply for a patrol job in the park. Between the two of them they've logged hundreds of hours on rescues in the park, and mentored the rangers who, come 2018, would point a writer in their direction as the spokesmen of choice on SAR.

And there's another thing about Robinson, which is a bit more difficult to parse because it has to do with poop. It also has as much to do with rescue in Denali as saving the lives of climbers in trouble, because it is about

Rangers and mountaineers come to Denali for these things: big mountains, wide-open spaces, and profound challenge.
DENALI NATIONAL PARK AND PRESERVE MUSEUM COLLECTIONS. PHOTO: PETER SANCHEZ

saving the mountain itself—and saving the experience of mountaineering, or just simply walking in the wilderness.

Robinson has long been focused on the issue of human-waste disposal in the park, and for good reason. Since the opening of the West Buttress route in 1951, the National Park Service estimates up to 215,000 pounds (or 97 metric tons) of poop have been deposited on, or in, the Kahiltna Glacier, where for decades mountaineers were encouraged to drop their business down crevasses. Robinson's worry, and that of others working on preservation of the mountain's ecosystems: At some point, decades down the line, thousands of blue bags full of poop are going to be squeezed out the toes of the glaciers ringing the mountain.

To mitigate the problem, Robinson came up with an innovative waste-collection technology known as the Clean Mountain Can (CMC), which can hold the fecal output of a single climber for the course of a typical expedition. You carry it in, sit on it when nature calls, and carry it out. Its creation and promotion have been transformative on Denali, and Robinson has been hailed as a hero of another kind for being its champion.

THE LESSONS OF 1967

Author Andy Hall opens *Denali's Howl*, his book about the disastrous 1967 Wilcox expedition, with a description of his father, Greg Hall, then superintendent of Mount McKinley National Park, scanning the sodden tundra below a storm-shrouded Denali. He spots something—a person, perhaps; a survivor. The elder Hall was many days into a complicated search-and-rescue operation that would ultimately fail. The subsequent recovery mission would also fail. Seven men died near the summit in a monster storm; all but two simply vanished.

Months earlier, in frigid February, another expedition ran into trouble on the peak. Given the season, this was not entirely unexpected. Members of the Davidson expedition knew they were in for one hell of a time attempting the first winter ascent of Denali, and sure enough, they encountered some of the wickedest storm conditions ever recorded.

The worst for the Davidson team came early on, when one of its members crashed through a snow bridge into a crevasse and perished. Despite the tragedy, the mountaineers persisted, only to encounter another kind of worst when the three-man summit team was pinned down for days by a fierce storm. Miraculously, unbelievably, the trio survived. Taking advantage of a weather window to continue their descent, they were spotted by a rescue helicopter, plucked from the route, and whisked to the safety of a hospital.

But in his memoir, *Minus 148°*, expedition leader Art Davidson describes his dismay when the rescue helicopter arrived. He and his teammates had survived nightmare days in a shallow, hand-dug cave just below the summit; they were starving and frostbitten. Still, Davidson felt they could make it off the mountain without assistance. They'd assumed the risk, and were willing to follow through.

These two expeditions and the rescues they engendered redefined a number of aspects of search and rescue on Denali and beyond in their aftermath. Buffeted by criticism and driven by their own sense of what was right and what was needed, park rangers and officials took a good, hard look at every cost, from the money spent on rescue efforts to the loss of human life.

The Wilcox expedition has inspired a small library of books and articles focusing on what went wrong and attempting to fix blame. Reading through the volumes of information and analysis, three things percolate:

First, the expedition got caught in a convergence of storm systems that proved devastating, not only on Denali but beyond the mountain and park. Incessant rainfall caused flooding along rivers throughout the region—the Teklanika, the Nenana, the Tanana, the Chena—and the flooding, in turn, caused significant property damage in Fairbanks and rural communities. There's no fix for bad weather, but improved weather forecasting techniques and technologies have come into play over the years, mitigating this unknown.

Second, the expedition was plagued by personality conflicts, which weakened the team's ability to rescue itself by undermining the mutual trust that plays such an important role in wilderness survival. Though the Davidson expedition also dealt with personality quirks and different levels of physical ability and experience, following the death of their teammate those remaining were forced to take a long, hard look at their motivations and relationships. If this happened in a corporate boardroom instead of an igloo complex on North America's highest peak, it could be called team-building. It's also now recognized as a critical component of any successful expedition.

DON'T PRESS IT UNLESS YOU MEAN IT

This is what happens on Denali when a climber triggers their InReach or SPOT device SOS, as described by South District ranger Tucker Chenoweth in a June 2016 Denali Dispatch. He was cautioning against accidental activations (in one case, a climber admitted he was "just testing" his device), but this sequence sets in motion whether the emergency is real or not:

1. The SOS button is activated.
2. An emergency message is sent to the International Emergency Response Coordination Center (IERCC) with global positioning system (GPS) coordinates and whatever information the person needing rescue has included in their profile.
3. The IERCC contacts the nearest local emergency response agency. For all Alaska's national parks, including Denali, the Alaska Region Communication Center (ARCC) is contacted.
4. The ARCC calls the South District Ranger-on-Call. If the Ranger-on-Call is not physically at the Walter Harper Talkeetna Ranger Station—say they're home with family—they must drive back to the station.
5. Field rangers at both the 7,200-foot base camp and the 14,200-foot camp are alerted, [as well as] rangers at the 17,200-foot camp if possible.
6. If the GPS coordinates of the activated device appear to originate in a main camp on Denali, the ranger patrol must contact each tent to locate the SOS callers.
7. As this is happening, resources in Talkeetna are called into the ranger station, including the helicopter pilot, other aviation resources (manager, mechanic), and other rangers.
8. The number of people involved continues to expand until the nature of the emergency is identified and resolved. This could involve up to twenty people for a false alarm—and more if going to a site outside a main camp is the only way to determine the nature of the incident.

If the incident is a false alarm, the action ends there. If it's not, rangers and emergency responders do whatever is necessary, possible, and safe to resolve the incident with no loss of life or limb.

Third, inadequate and/or confusing technologies and policies conspired to muddle search-and-rescue efforts. This is where concrete steps could be, and have been, taken in the years since. All the elements that now play into successful search and rescue on Denali and elsewhere in the state—a clear chain of command, optimal radio communications, National Park Service regulations, expectations, and educational programs, state-of-the-art aeronautics and weather-forecasting technologies—got a once-over in the wake of the catastrophe.

The lessons of 1967, both successes and failures, continue to inform. Modern technology and the speed of life Outside has brought change fast and hard to adventure throughout Alaska. Summiters have long coveted the Denali "first," from the flurry of turn-of-the-twentieth-century expeditions to modern-day alpinists seeking to be the fastest, the oldest, the youngest, the whatever in whichever category has an opening. But claiming a first in any set time frame—a vacation window that lasts, say, two weeks, three weeks, even a month—applies pressures on climbers the mountain has no sympathy for. That means climbers may be inspired to make dangerous pushes through inclement conditions or beyond personal physical limits. A weather window on Denali is shaped by Denali, not by any forecaster, after all. Not everyone acclimates to altitude at the same rate, and some don't acclimate at all. The desire to be first doesn't alter reality.

How the lessons of 1967 apply to newer challenges on the mountain—distractions like tweeting and blogging about ascents in real time, and the expectations that accompany the cell phone—have yet to be seen. It can be argued aspiring climbers nowadays, documenting their climbs as they go, are displaying a dangerous new kind of bravado, conflating arrival on the mountain with success, and are distracted from the task at hand. It can be argued the questions of temperament and expectation remain as real for modern expeditions as they did for the members of the Wilcox expedition.

Underestimating the amplified forces of nature anywhere in Alaska, and especially in Alaska's mountains, is well recognized as a factor in bad decision-making and bad outcomes. "The mountain doesn't care about your airline ticket or your social media," Miller points out. But

Denali is perfectly capable of throwing a climber's strengths and weaknesses into sharp focus, outlined in brilliant sunlight piercing a hard blue northern sky.

Cosmic Ray

———

The glacier was the same as ever, a thing of white magnifi-
cence, and a thing to be watched out for every second.
—GRANT PEARSON REFLECTING ON DENALI'S MULDROW
GLACIER IN *MY LIFE OF HIGH ADVENTURE*

On June 7, 1913, four men finally reached the summit of Denali. Their climb followed on years of competitive and sometimes contentious attempts by well-heeled adventurers from the East Coast. After weeks of wearying effort ferrying supplies up the crevassed Muldrow Glacier and braving frigid temperatures and gales that pinned them to the mountainside, Harry Karstens, Walter Harper, Hudson Stuck, and Robert Tatum finally stood atop the roof of North America.

For nearly two decades after, no one tried again.

The long climbing drought was broken in 1932. Two teams set their sights on the summit, working somewhat in tandem. Both expeditions followed the same route as the Stuck expedition, ascending the Muldrow Glacier, on the north side of the 20,310-foot peak, and then the Harper Glacier, named for the first man on top, a native Alaskan. Along the way the nine men notched a number of mountaineering firsts. They also established an enduring search-and-rescue legacy—that of one team coming to the aid of a second when circumstances go south.

The Lindley-Liek expedition was headlined by Harry Liek, superintendent of what was then known as Mount McKinley National Park. Coleader Alfred Lindley, the park's chief ranger, Grant Pearson, and a Norwegian ski mountaineer named Erling Strom rounded out the team. Their goal was to ski the mountain top to bottom. That effort failed, but the team succeeded in tagging both the high point on the South Peak as well as Denali's North Peak. The Lindley-Liek team was the first to reach the two back-to-back.

The primary mission of the second team, the Cosmic Ray expedition, was to conduct scientific experiments on the mountain, but they, too, hoped to reach the summit. The subject of study? You guessed it: cosmic rays. Understanding the behavior of the rays at high latitudes and altitudes presented an intriguing question, and Denali posed an intriguing target. Arthur Compton, a physicist with the University of Chicago who'd earned a Nobel Prize for his work in the field, recruited a thirty-eight-year-old electrical engineer named Allan Carpé to lead a team to the peak to learn more. Carpé, in turn, recruited twenty-eight-year-old Theodore Koven, another accomplished mountaineer and scientist; Edward Beckwith, also a researcher; Percy Olton; and Nicholas Spadavecchia to assist. Compton did not make the climb.

Carpé's résumé was impressive. It included long tenure with Bell Telephone Laboratories, but he also had a solid record as an alpinist, having climbed a number of northern latitude peaks including Mount Fairweather in what is now Glacier Bay National Park and Preserve. His mountaineering peers praised him as a competent and thoughtful climber: "He had great self-confidence and unusual courage and daring," wrote W. S. Ladd in the *American Alpine Journal*. "He was not a rapid goer, nor did he show speed in step-cutting. All his efforts I shall always think of as being governed by one motive—precision."

Both expeditions were underway by late April, and though Olton and Spadavecchia (called Spad) were delayed a few days in traveling to Mount McKinley, all of the men had made their way onto the Muldrow Glacier by the first days of May. The park's sled dogs, with the permission of Superintendent Liek, were harnessed to transport some of the Cosmic Ray team's eight hundred pounds of scientific equipment to their research camp at the head of the glacier. Transporting the rest of the team's twelve hundred pounds of gear onto the mountain, as well as the teammates themselves, set one of the most significant precedents in the art and science of climbing, and of search and rescue in Alaska: the use of aircraft.

The aeronautics were spectacular. A bush pilot with "long experience" named Joe Crosson, who seemed to Beckwith "unconcerned at the prospect of attempting to land on the untried slope[s] of McKinley," was employed to ferry both gear and men onto the Muldrow. Aviation firsts on Denali are as dramatic as climbing firsts, and with his pioneering landing on the Muldrow, Crosson set a high bar. On April 25, with the mountaintop wreathed in cloud, the pilot deposited Carpé and Beckwith on the glacier at about six thousand feet, the first ever such landing. Beckwith noted the elevation was better than the two had hoped for. From his vantage on the slopes above, Pearson observed the event, writing, "I'll never forget the thrill of that moment, standing there fifteen thousand feet above sea level, watching a plane fly several thousand feet below us. I knew, then, how an eagle must feel."

But Crosson's success wasn't without mishap. After making the drop, the pilot took off for home but, unable to gain sufficient speed and altitude to stay airborne, was forced to set his plane down on a snowfield out of sight of the Cosmic Ray camp. "With no good-byes he disappeared in the whirling snow up the glacier," Beckwith wrote. "It was a long time before he left the ice. . . . We saw that he did get into the air. We waited to hear him overhead as he would naturally circle and fly back. There was no sound but the blowing wind and we concluded he had probably crashed."

It wasn't a crash exactly. Crosson was fine. His single-engine Fairchild was fine, just temporarily unable to get off the ground. The pilot donned snowshoes and descended back to the camp to enlist the help of the mountaineers. Despite what could be construed as catastrophic, Crosson was "calm and matter-of-course," and the group sat down over a meal of canned beans to contemplate a plan of action. The next morning the pilot, with the help of Beckwith and Carpé, freed the plane from its bed of ice and Crosson flew back to Fairbanks to pick up the other team members, Spadavecchia and Olton.

While the Lindley-Liek expedition made its assault on Denali's twin summits, Carpé and Koven set the high camp at the head of the Muldrow Glacier in order and got to work. The tents were erected. The gear was organized. The cosmic ray equipment was assembled and Carpé began taking readings. The team received an airdrop of supplies from Crosson on May 3, the pilot diving at the camp and pushing the packages out of the plane's open door. The two men skied down to retrieve the goods, and unpacking the food and spare gear felt like Christmas Eve at eleven thousand feet, Koven wrote in his diary.

Over the next couple of days, the two scientist/mountaineers moved up and down the head of the Muldrow, ferrying goods between camps and conducting readings via trails that seemed safer with each successful passage. Their diaries contain notes about fine conditions and weather, though warming conditions raised some concern that the snow bridges spanning crevasses might be softening.

No one can be certain about what exactly transpired on or about May 9. What is known is that on May 10 the Lindley-Liek team, on descent from its successful climb, was hammered. They'd bagged two summits in two days, enduring Denali's fickle weather and thin air in the doing. They'd handled a near disastrous fall between the peaks as well, when Pearson took a long slide on a slope below Denali's south summit. The incident left the climber bloodied—he impaled his arm with his ice ax as he self-arrested—but not incapacitated.

Now, at the head of the Muldrow, the rattled and exhausted summiters stumbled into the empty, orderly Cosmic Ray camp. Packs and sleeping bags were inside the tents, but the occupants could not be hailed. The circumstances were unusual, ominous. After a quick meal, the team continued down the mountain. A mile and a half farther on they found Theodore Koven, dead of exposure amid his wandering tracks. Carpé was nowhere to be found.

Mystified by the circumstances, the Lindley-Liek teammates did what they could. They bound Koven's body to a sledge recovered from the camp above and gave up the search for Carpé, resuming their descent. But conditions on the glacier were hazardous and the dead man's mode of transport cumbersome. The climbers hadn't traveled far before a crevasse opened under Grant Pearson. He plunged forty feet into a "black, bottomless" darkness, and came to rest on a plug of snow between unforgiving walls of ice. His companions threw him a rope; hand over hand, the ranger was able to haul himself to safety.

"That crevasse was the loneliest spot I've ever been in," Pearson recalled.

Recognizing the danger posed to the living by recovery of the dead, the team decided to leave Koven on the mountain, wrapping him in a tent, burying him in snow, and erecting the sledge to mark his temporary resting place. His remains would be recovered months later by another expedition.

Not much farther downslope, the summiters discovered a pair of crampons and an ice ax at the rim of another deep crevasse. There the mystery began to unravel, as much as it could.

Considering the scene—ski tracks, footfalls, the final disposition of the younger scientist—the Lindley-Liek crew figured Carpé and Koven were traveling together and headed down the glacier when the accident occurred. Unroped and following a route they'd traveled before, it was assumed Koven, on skis, cleared the killer crevasse but Carpé, on foot, broke through a weakened snow bridge and tumbled into the void. Attempting to rescue his partner, Koven sidestepped to the brink and then fell in as well. He was injured but somehow, probably over many long, cold hours, was able to extract himself. Despondent, hurting, and exhausted, the younger climber stumbled back toward the Cosmic Ray high camp, but only made it a few hundred yards before perishing of exposure on the surface of the glacier.

Pearson, who went on to accumulate a wealth of experience, respect, and love for Denali in his decades of service as a ranger and superintendent in the national park, reflected on the accident this way in his memoir, *My Life of High Adventure*:

> *The story was plainly written in the snow, a stark tragedy of two men, supposedly experienced mountaineers, betrayed by their eagerness to greet their friends. They had gone down the glacier unroped, over a trail they thought they knew, and one of the mountain's oldest traps had sprung shut on them as it almost had on me.*

Meanwhile, lower down on Denali, a separate search-and-rescue scenario was developing. At the Cosmic Ray expedition's lower camp, Beckwith had taken ill. He first attributed his malaise to canned chicken, which had also caused Spad and Olton some upset. To remain on schedule—they had a date to keep with Carpé and Koven at the high camp—the group decided to split up, with Spad and Olton heading to the first icefall on the Muldrow, and Beckwith planning to follow when he felt better.

He didn't. His condition worsening, Beckwith set out his skis in an X, signaling his distress, and hoped his partners would see the sign. They didn't. The sick man, feverish, in pain, and unable to eat, fended for himself for nearly two days, until Olton returned to retrieve more supplies for the icefall cache.

Assessing Beckwith's deteriorating condition, Olton hailed Spad, and together the men retreated to the main Cosmic Ray camp—the "big tent"—down near McGonagall Pass. From there Spad, his seventy-pound pack loaded with enough supplies to last six days, set out for Stony Creek, where he hoped to be able to call for a plane to pick up his ailing comrade. But, Beckwith observed later, "Maps of the region had proved very inaccurate, and Spad had to depend on his general knowledge of the country, which of course was very fragmentary." Olton stayed in camp to help Beckwith.

When the Lindley-Liek team finally arrived at the McGonagall camp, they found Beckwith completely incapacitated, Olton in caregiving mode … and Spadavecchia overdue. They delivered the bad news about Carpé and Koven, then considered the options for rescue of the rest of the Cosmic Ray team. Superintendent Liek and ranger Pearson, with their firsthand knowledge of the lay of Denali's land, took the lead. They were able to get down to civilization quickly and initiate rescue for the survivors.

Still, there were complications. The quickly advancing Alaskan spring meant planes based in Fairbanks were taking off in entirely different conditions than they'd encounter on the slopes of Denali. In the lowlands they were outfitted with wheels, but skis were required for the highland glaciers. The solution was simple, ingenious, and another first: Fairbanks's fire department sprayed gallons of water onto the city's airfield, turning it into what Pearson called a "manmade mud pie," slick and suitable for both takeoff and landing on skis. On May 16, Beckwith was airlifted from the mountain and deposited safely in a hospital. He made a complete recovery.

But Spad was still missing, and Olton remained in camp in the event the climber-turned-hiker should return. Liek dispatched rangers on foot to look for the missing man, and the Fairbanks airfield was flooded again so another plane, this one a Stearman piloted by Robbie Robbins, could locate Spad from the skies, and bring him and Olton back to civilization.

Olton's pickup was the first order of business but even that didn't go as expected: Upon landing, the skis on Robbins's plane froze to the ice. To free the ship Olton rocked the wings while the pilot ran the propeller at full throttle—which succeeded in breaking an axle and stranding the men in place.

Now, after days of uncertainty and hardship, came good news: While Olton and Robbins awaited their own rescue, Spadavecchia saved himself. "At ten o'clock that night," Beckwith explained in his account of the expedition, "Olton heard a call which was surprisingly similar to one which he and Spad had used to signal each other. Looking out, he saw Spad coming over the pass."

Olton and Robbins welcomed the wanderer who, despite having rambled in Denali's formidable wilderness for ten days, was only "somewhat exhausted . . . but in good shape." Spad had ranged many miles in the backcountry, conserving his supplies and supplementing meals with porcupine he speared using a ski pole. When he couldn't find Stony Creek, where he'd hope to hail help, he'd wisely turned around and retraced his steps to the Cosmic Ray base camp.

Meantime, back in Fairbanks, when the pilot Robbins didn't return as expected, another plane took to the air, this one equipped with wheels and with pilot Jerry Jones at the controls. Once he located Robbins's missing plane, Jones dropped a can of lampblack to the flyer on the glacier; the stranded pilot spelled out "S & O SAFE AXLE BROKE" in the white snow. With that information—S & O standing for Spadavecchia and Olton—Jones promptly turned around, flew back to Fairbanks, picked up a replacement axle for the Stearman, and returned to make the drop.

Robbins repaired the plane in the field but ended up flying off Denali alone; even with the axle replaced, he determined the craft wasn't strong enough to safely carry both himself and two passengers. Upon his return, Alaska Airlines, the company behind the pilots, decided it had had enough of flying to Denali that season. Given that both Olton and Spad were able-bodied, they were guided out of the wild on foot, eighty miles to McKinley Park Station, by national park rangers.

The deaths of Carpé and Koven were the first recorded on the mountain, and that legacy remains etched on the landscape. A pair of peaks in the shadow of Denali and overlooking the Muldrow bear their names. Another peak in the Alaska Range is named for pioneering pilot Joe Crosson. The mountains are a fitting symbol for the close connections of climbers, rangers, and pilots as adventurers, heroes, and rescuers—connections forged in the early days of mountaineering in Denali.

The Long Wait: The Thayer Expedition

Of Elton Thayer it could be said that climbing to him was a deep spiritual experience rather than a mere struggle to accumulate as many ascents or impress others with his feats. He climbed because he loved the mountains and not because he wanted publicity, acclaim, or recognition.
—THAYER EXPEDITION MEMBER MORTON WOOD

As far as Mount McKinley National Park was concerned, ranger Elton Thayer and his team were primed to climb Denali. "Your expedition appears to be well organized and equipped for this undertaking," Superintendent Grant Pearson noted, and he would know: Pearson was part of the Lindley-Liek expedition of 1932, the first team to summit both Denali's North and South Peaks.

Twenty-seven-year-old Thayer assembled a solid crew of mountaineers for the climb, including twenty-five-year-old Corporal George Argus, stationed at the Big Delta Arctic Indoctrination School; Leslie Viereck, a soldier stationed at Fort Richardson out of Anchorage; and Morton Wood, husband of legendary Alaskan flyer Ginny Wood and one of the operators of Camp Denali, a tourist destination near Wonder Lake and the small mining community of Kantishna, at the end of about ninety miles of rough park road. Thayer and Viereck both had big Arctic mountain ascents under their belts, Argus was a climbing instructor, and Wood called the spectacular terrain on the north side of McKinley Park his backyard. They were young, strong, experienced, and eager to explore.

They were also well outfitted. Included in the equipment Pearson referenced were tents sewn by Thayer's wife, Bernice, of sturdy olive drab upholstery fabric with reinforced seams and parachute cord tie-downs, which Morton Wood claimed "worked out excellently through the entire trip and showed no sign of wear, despite hard usage and strong winds." Ginny Wood was recruited to make a supply drop to the climbers once they reached their base camp on the Ruth Glacier—"30 days' rations and all our high-altitude climbing equipment." On the long approach to the south-side glacier, the four climbers hefted packs loaded with seventy to eighty pounds of supplies, sustenance and gear that doubled as good training wait.

The expedition's goal was to complete the first traverse of Denali, climbing up one side of the mountain and down the other. The trek began on April 17, 1954, with the four men beginning a fifty-mile snowshoe slog from Curry through river valleys clogged with willow and sticky spring snow to the Ruth Glacier, a forty-mile-long river of ice on the southeast side of the Denali massif. Base camp for the summit attempt was in the Great Basin of the Ruth, located above the Great Gorge where the glacier, more than thirty-seven hundred feet thick, is pinched between cliffs five thousand feet high.

From base camp the team continued up the fractured glacier toward the unclimbed South Buttress, ferrying caches and encountering stupendous icefalls as they climbed. They confronted violent winds and fatigue, avalanche danger and bitter cold, route-finding difficulties and blizzards that confined them to their tents for days. They laboriously chipped footholds into one ice field, creating what they dubbed a "Commuter's Trail" up the "Lotsa Face" (think Mount Everest's Lohtse Face, which was summited for the first time the year before). The staircase they created had more than a thousand steps, advancing up and across the interminable ice slope. All this they took in stride, to be expected on a first ascent exploring unknown terrain on a mountain like Denali.

They also encountered the sublime: Views of the summit and surrounding peaks that lifted their hearts, Mounts Foraker and Crosson shining like diamonds; a "fantastic formation" of ice forming a cornice that Wood described as an "overhanging glacier"; a "weird cave" of "cold blue ice blocks" where the climber expected to find stalagmites and stalactites, as a spelunker might in a limestone cave.

The Great Gorge of the Ruth Glacier in Denali National Park and Preserve.
COURTESY OF THE NATIONAL PARK SERVICE

Undaunted and amazed, the Thayer expedition forged a route to the high pass that would permit their descent down the north slopes of the mountain. They would not have to retreat, which was cause for celebration—the traverse was possible. And the summit was within a day's hike—a hike the climbers completed on May 15.

The team descended from the mountaintop to their high camp at 17,200 feet and settled in overnight. The next morning Thayer and company set off down the Harper Glacier, which descends Denali's north face toward the Muldrow Glacier. This could be considered the easy way down: It was part of the standard route at the time, following the "trail" blazed by the first ascent team in 1913, Pearson's team in 1932, and others before the ascendancy of the West Buttress route from the Kahiltna Glacier.

Snow conditions deteriorated at the Cockscomb, where the climbers had to traverse "deep snow over ice." They proceeded as carefully as they could, with one climber moving down while the other three on the rope belayed him. At 12,800 feet, the climbers arrived at a "steep, nasty pitch," where they discovered a rope fixed with pickets by another team. Hitching into what could be considered additional protection—a decision considered dubious by mountaineer and Denali expert Bradford Washburn in hindsight—the men continued to descend, strung together with Argus in the lead and Thayer at the rear.

Then Elton Thayer slipped. His fall couldn't be arrested by any of his companions given the uncompromising snow conditions. The fixed rope, despite its promise, offered no protection at all; it broke loose as the alpinists, one after the other, pitched down the mountainside. Wood likened the slide to taking a fall while skiing in powder, except "it seemed to last for an eternity." The four men slid nearly a thousand feet before reaching a slope that was less steep. There, Viereck plunged into a crevasse, and anchored his companions.

It was over. "Then suddenly silence," Wood recalled, "except for the gentle hiss of the snow that was still in motion all around me."

George Argus was seated in the snow uphill from Wood. Leslie Viereck was standing in the snow higher above, dazed. Elton Thayer was dangling by the rope over a fifteen-foot ice cliff. He was dead, his back broken in the fall.

Aside from being banged up and "in a state of shock," Wood and Viereck emerged from the slide relatively unscathed (though Viereck suffered "rib injuries"). George Argus was a different story. His companions feared at first both his hips were broken, but when all was said and done it was only one hip, which was dislocated. His knees were battered, and he'd sustained chest and head trauma—his front teeth had been "pushed in" and his face was "badly bruised."

The team's gear—packs, sleeping bags, clothing—was scattered across the slope in the fall. Wood and Viereck gathered what they could, including one of the tents, sleeping bags, an air mattress, and Thayer's pack, then etched a flat spot in the slope, set up the tent, and settled inside with their injured partner. A quick meal, then the three men fell into what could only have been a troubled sleep.

Because of Argus's injuries, the climbers remained at their exposed high camp for the next six days, hoping Wood's wife, Ginny, would fly over and see their distress signal stamped in the snow. Ginny was aloft and searching, but not where her husband and his teammates were camped; she had no way of knowing the climbers had completed the traverse, and was focused on the south side of the mountain. When it became clear an air rescue wasn't likely, the men decided to save themselves. "Anyone looking at this slope from below would rightly conclude that it was too hazardous," Wood wrote. "More lives would only be endangered, and after all we had gotten ourselves into this mess and it was up to us to find a way out of it."

Wood and Viereck stomped a path across the snowy slope and down to the Muldrow, a trail to safety. They wrapped Argus in sleeping bags and the tent, fashioning a kind of litter. Wood marked Elton Thayer's resting place with his pack board, so that his remains could, hopefully, be recovered one day. That would never come to pass; the climber remains on the mountain. Then the two healthier climbers ferried the injured man down to much welcomed "flat ice" at the head of the Muldrow.

Once a new camp was established on the glacier, the team grappled with a hard decision. Argus was in no shape to aid in his rescue, and Wood and Viereck couldn't handle the evacuation on their own. But Argus was well enough to fend for himself if he stayed in the tent. The men decided Wood and Viereck would head down for help, and Argus would remain on the mountain until they returned. The two healthy climbers made sure their mate had everything he needed to survive: enough food and fuel for ten days, access to the stove, and an improvised bedpan, then bid him farewell.

A long march down the heavily crevassed Muldrow, then over McGonagall Pass and across the McKinley River, was broken only when the men stopped to catch four hours' sleep and munch on a "Logan" bar—the 1950s version of a Clif Bar. When they reached a backcountry cabin stocked with food and supplies by Thayer himself, they napped and ate breakfast. They hoped to meet a car that would drive them down to park headquarters, but the park road, snowbound through the winter, was still closed. Disheartened and exhausted, Wood bemoaned the idea that they'd have to keep walking for two reasons: Argus's rescue would be delayed, and the 85 miles they'd have to add to their trek, after already logging 130 miles in their successful traverse.

Before heading down the park highway, Wood and Viereck turned toward Kantishna, where at least one old prospector, Johnny Busia, might be able to help. Resting in Busia's cabin they got lucky: The park super-intendent, Grant Pearson, and his chief ranger just happened to punch through the last snow banks on the park road in a Dodge Power Wagon, arriving in the one-time boomtown not long after the mountaineers. Their ride back to civilization was hitched.

Argus's rescue was set in motion immediately. Being an enlisted man, the military spared no resources to get him off the mountain as quickly as possible. The Seventy-Fourth Air Rescue Squadron, based in Fair-banks, was mobilized. Still, the task was daunting. The Muldrow is mas-sive, Denali is enormous, and Wood and Viereck, bruised, battered, and exhausted, were unable to pinpoint the exact location of the handmade tent and the man inside.

The army plan called for a small party, including Dr. John McCall, a veteran climber of Denali and professor at the University of Alaska; Fred Milan, one of Argus's former climbing companions; and a handful of enlisted men from the Indoctrination Center in Big Delta, to be flown onto the Muldrow as an advance team. Deposited at about six thousand feet, and supported by airdrops of supplies, including a sled for Argus's eventual transport off the glacier, the advance team would make a "forced march" up the glacier to the one-man camp at its head. A base of operations in sup-port of the rescue mission, supplied both by air and via the park road, was established at Wonder Lake; the air base of operations was at the airfield near Lake Minchumina, north and west of the park.

Argus, meantime, was diligently surviving. He rationed his food care-fully, read, and by one account mapped features on the landscape he could see through his open tent flap. He remained unable to move his legs with-out pain, much less walk. He was heartened by the sound of aircraft flying overhead as the days went on, knowing they were part of the rescue effort. Argus displayed, Dr. McCall told a newspaper reporter, "a tremendous amount of plain old American guts."

Weather kept airships grounded for a couple of days at the rescue's out-set, but on May 27 a pilot flying an L-20 located a "hole in the clouds" and spotted tracks he thought belonged to McCall and Milan, who had been airlifted onto the glacier two days before. He dropped a sled near the trail.

Later that morning a helicopter was able to fly low enough for two more rescuers to jump out onto the glacier. Another helicopter, delivering two more men, encountered some difficulty in the drop-off. "Due to a misunderstanding on signals," an army report records, one of the men was unable to jump from the copter onto the ice, "and was left hanging by his hands from the litter rack as the pilot made a complete circle of the glacier at an altitude of about 150 feet." That rescuer was deposited safely onto the Muldrow on the second pass.

A base camp was established and five men, led by Dr. McCall, set off in roped teams up the glacier. The Muldrow was devious: Its yawning crevasses, which had worried Wood and Viereck on their descent, were now obscured by two feet of freshly fallen snow, and each of the rescuers would take a plunge into the void at some point as they passed through the first icefall. They set up a support camp and received an airdrop of supplies, then settled in for the night.

The crevasse maze of the second icefall presented more challenges as McCall and company continued up toward Argus's bivouac the next day. Encountering an apparent "cul-de-sac," a pair of the enlisted men made a "brilliant reconnaissance" to find the way around a huge fissure. The rescuers ended their day at 10,500 feet, establishing a high camp. Several airdrops of supplies were required to outfit the camp, since one of the loads landed in a crevasse. The army also had to drop another sled. It turned out the first was dropped near what were now believed to be the descending tracks of Wood and Viereck, which had since been buried in snow. This meant locating Argus would be that much harder, "like trying to find a snowball in a snowstorm."

But the team was successful. On May 30, McCall and Milan reached Argus. Although his injuries had, in the words of one rescuer, rendered the young man "helpless … he needs a doctor in the worst way," Argus was stable and alert, and even offered McCall and company some tea. The rescuers loaded him into the sled and moved him down to the high camp, where the team rested and helped defrost and stabilize the summiter for the rest of the long trek down the glacier. But Argus's condition was deteriorating; when morning came, McCall administered morphine to ease his discomfort. The climber was evacuated by sled to McGonagall Pass, then airlifted to the hospital in Fairbanks. The rescuers were airlifted off the mountain as well, and by June 1, Denali's aprons were clean of search and rescue. For a while, at least.

Though Elton Thayer's death casts a long shadow on the expedition that bears his name, what he and his comrades accomplished in those long days on Denali is momentous in mountaineering circles. The team completed the first traverse of the High One, as well as the first ascent from the south side, an aspect that had stymied three previous expeditions. Likewise, the remarkable effort to get George Argus off the mountain safely covered new ground in search and rescue. The coordination of teams on the glacier and in the air, pooling military, civilian, and park service resources, laid the groundwork for modern SAR efforts on Denali and elsewhere in Alaska.

After Elton Thayer died, his wife, Bernice, discovered she was pregnant with his son, whom she named for his father. Many years later, when the surviving climbers, Bernice, and young Elton gathered to remember the climb, she echoed the sentiments of Morton Wood, written not long after the accident.

"This was not a group of mountaineers out to conquer the mountain, waving their ice picks," she told her local newspaper. "This was more of them communing with nature and sharing the beauty. They did it to enjoy the experience of climbing and the camaraderie."

Rescues of the Rich and Famous:
John Day and the Whittakers

———

All sorts of things went wrong on the McKinley climb.
—LOU WHITTAKER, *MEMOIRS OF A MOUNTAIN GUIDE*

Six days into what was, at the time, the most elaborate rescue operation ever staged on Denali, more than thirty climbers hunkered down on the Kahiltna Glacier waiting for the weather to clear. Among the stranded: Lou and Jim Whittaker. Natives of Washington State, the twin brothers had honed their skills on Mount Rainier, the stunning alpine test piece looming over Seattle's metropolitan area. They had yet to become legendary: Jim Whittaker would be the first American to stand atop Mount Everest in 1963, and Lou helped pioneer Everest's North Col route in 1968. But in May 1960, the brothers were simply battered successful Denali summiters, still stuck on the mountain after their climb had disintegrated with a single slip on descent.

The Whittaker brothers' journey to Denali, however, was based on their growing reputations as first-rate mountaineers and guides. In the late 1950s and early 1960s the twins were at the top of their games, honing alpine skills in the imposing Cascades and on peaks in neighboring Canada, and expanding their scope as finances and growing families allowed. They'd cultivated significant friendships in the strong climbing community that flourished in the Pacific Northwest, home turf for well-known and long-lived clubs like the Mountaineers and the Mazamas. They weren't dirtbag climbers, like those who would later push the limits in Yosemite, but their calling hadn't yet translated into the big bucks.

John Day was another story. Reflecting on his association with Day in *Memoirs of a Mountain Guide*, Lou Whittaker describes the man, hailing from Medford, Oregon, as a middle-aged "millionaire rancher." His fortune in hand, Day had shifted his focus from making it big in the business world to climbing big mountains. He sought out the Whittakers to guide him on record-breaking summit assaults throughout Washington and Canada. Now he wanted to stand atop the roof of North America. He'd foot the bill.

It didn't take much to convince young Lou Whittaker to join the team, and Lou recruited Jim to help shoulder the load. The fourth man on the team was Pete Schoening, another top-notch alpinist whose reputation was sealed on an attempt to climb K2 in 1953. When one member of the expedition slipped and his rope tangled with those of the others, Schoening singlehandedly held the anchor rope and the six men attached to it, averting disaster.

Rainier is arguably as treacherous as Denali. Though significantly lower in height, at 14,411 feet, and at a less northerly latitude, the peak is streaked with glaciers that shed rock and ice in avalanches and slides on a regular basis. On its north side the mountain boasts steep walls that pose route-finding challenges for the best climbers, and when it's not beset by storms blowing in off the Pacific, Rainier is fully capable of conjuring its own whiteout conditions and freezing temperatures. The Whittakers, having cut their teeth on the capricious volcano, had some idea about what they were getting into on Denali. Anything could happen. They were prepared.

But the point, for Day, was to set a speed record. Though the dangers of not acclimating to altitude on Denali are well documented and can strike even the strongest climbers, the team decided to skip the weeks' long camp-by-camp process of a traditional assault, and opted to climb "alpine style."

To accomplish this flash assault, the Day expedition had to rely on airdrops of supplies. And to do that, they needed to figure out a way around a park regulation that reserved the use of multiple airdrops for expeditions conducting scientific research. In correspondence with the park, Day asserted his expedition's intent to gather data on glaciers. Moreover, Day secured a letter from the American Geographical Society not only supporting the team's glaciological inquiries—"photographic interpretation, meteorological observation and physical measurement of superficial features on the glacier"—but also touting its mountaineering expertise.

The Day expedition wasn't alone in using scientific subterfuge to expedite their summit aspirations; in those years teams frequently claimed they'd be conducting experiments to skirt the park requirement. And the park was hip to the tactic, as indicated in a note from the acting regional director stating, "We believe [Day's] interest in glacier measurements stems to a large degree as an effort to gain all support for his expedition." That said, Day and Jim Whittaker did document the Kahiltna and Peters Glaciers on the climb, taking photographs from various vantage points as they made their way up the mountain.

The assault began with pilot Don Sheldon of Talkeetna depositing Jim Whittaker and a load of supplies at 10,200 feet on May 14. John Day was flown in next; Lou Whittaker and Pete Schoening, with more supplies, were airlifted onto the Kahiltna last. Sheldon made another supply drop at 14,300 feet, where the expedition created another camp.

Over the next two days, the Day expedition moved quickly upward, using a fixed rope set by a Japanese party to gain the ridge of the West Buttress, and passing a team of five climbers from Anchorage in the process. Climber Helga Bading, part of the Anchorage team, recalled the four men raced by "without stopping to say hello, just a little bit." Jim Whittaker, on the other hand, notes he and his partners stopped and "chatted" with the other climbers as they passed.

The Anchorage and Seattle teams leapfrogged each other on May 17—summit day—when the Day party experienced what Jim Whittaker described as route-finding difficulties, enabling the crew from Anchorage to top out first. No matter; it was all good on top. Views from the summit, Jim Whittaker remembered, were "beautiful. Alaska boasts some of the most magnificent mountain scenery in the world and we enjoyed it immensely."

On the descent, any friendly competition that existed between the two teams took a backseat: Denali was dishing up challenges. The four men of the Anchorage squad—Paul Crews, Chuck Metzger, Andy Brauchli, and Dr. Rod Wilson—had left teammate Bading behind in their camp at 16,400 feet. She was suffering from acute mountain sickness, which would deteriorate into high-altitude cerebral edema (HACE), a buildup of fluid on the brain that can be fatal.

For the Day expedition, the trouble started at about seventeen thousand feet. Members of the Seattle team don't pinpoint blame for who started the slide in their official reports, for what Schoening called "obvious reasons"— though the climber does make the point that the older and less experienced John Day was not the first to slide. It was Jim Whittaker, according to the official account in the *American Alpine Journal*. Hard ice precipitated his slip on the slope below the pass.

The four men, each unable to arrest the fall, careened four hundred feet down the mountain. Wilson of the Anchorage team noticed the climbers all on the same rope, "piled at the bottom of a steep stretch." When they came to a stop and recovered their senses (or mostly recovered them, as it turned out), they called out to the Anchorage team for help and set about assessing the damage.

"On the way down I think I hit every angle of the compass, and felt my left leg break," John Day recalled. He was debilitated, unable to continue the descent on his own. Jim Whittaker, dazed and in shock but functional, helped his teammates "stuff" Day into a sleeping bag. They then anchored the injured man to the slope with ice axes, making sure he was secure before they continued to their high camp to pick up supplies. Paul Crews from the Anchorage team, which had also retreated to the Seattle team's camp, brought a tent up to the bivouac site, slit a hole in its floor, and raised it over the injured man.

As the Whittaker brothers and Schoening descended, they divested themselves of the rope that connected them and continued independent of each other. Jim got to camp first; he was unsteady on the slope, repeatedly stumbling and falling. He crawled into a sleeping bag and took stock, feeling bruised through the chest and experiencing difficulty breathing. Lou arrived next, sore and shaken, but otherwise OK. Schoening was nowhere to be seen. He'd been knocked unconscious in the fall and, according to Lou, was slow to recover his senses; his head injury, as it turned out, was significant enough that he wouldn't remember anything for ten to twelve hours after the slide. Despite the amnesia, Schoening retained his "climbing coordination and strength," which was enough for Lou and Jim to think he was completely lucid in the immediate aftermath of the event. But without the guidance of the rope or his comrades, Schoening wandered off course. When Lou found him he was curled on a rock ledge, with one glove missing and his exposed hand partially frostbitten. Lou led the disoriented man back to the camp.

"Here a lesson is to be learned," Jim Whittaker wrote later, reflecting on the incident. "We did not realize Pete was not completely rational since his conversation and action seemed to be normal. We were lucky nothing more serious happened to him and are thankful his expert skill and knowledge of mountains were imbedded in his subconscious."

The Anchorage team was able to make contact with authorities via the small radio they'd carried up the mountain. They relayed a message requesting evacuation of both Bading and Day. The Seattle teammates gathered supplies and climbed back up to where Day was anchored, setting up a camp at seventeen thousand feet. Day did all he could to expedite his own rescue, not pulling "any punches in using any means and influence I could to get help." He insisted messages be sent to the head of the Oregon Rescue Group, the governor of Oregon, an Alaskan guide with a "jet helicopter," and President Dwight Eisenhower, "having had previous contact with all four." He suspected his outreach was effective, because the military "gave us unlimited assistance, and the state of Alaska went 'all out' in helping."

The Alaska Rescue Group (ARG; now known as Alaska Mountain Rescue Group) had been organized a scant month before the massive operation on Denali began. The group mobilized immediately. The Rescue Coordination Center at Elmendorf Air Force Base also geared up, as did the Civil Air Patrol. When the Seattle-based Mountain Rescue Council received word of the accident via radio, it joined the effort as well. The Whittakers, after all, were kin.

From the start, the rescue effort was hampered by bad weather. Rain and low clouds nearly stymied the pilots flying in from Anchorage, who had to cruise low enough to follow the Alaska Railroad's tracks toward the park. While army helicopters and aircraft were converging on the airfield at Summit, along the rail line near the village of Cantwell, Don Sheldon took to the skies, hoping to pinpoint the location of the high camp where Day and his team were sheltering. He was unable to do so at first, so the incident commander dispatched a pair of helicopters, an H-37 and a HUIA. The HUIA, a nimble little copter, climbed to 17,500 feet and circled the peak, but was unable to locate the camp—and then its battery exploded in flight, forcing it out of commission.

Sheldon, however, was eventually able to find the bivouac and drop supplies. When the rescue effort resumed the next day, he was also able to guide the helicopters back to the site to evacuate the injured. Overnight, "the mountain was bombarded with tents, stoves and medical supplies from USAF C-123's," according to John Johnston, the ARG's chairman. The medical supplies were critical because on the mountain Helga Bading was deteriorating, "out of her head."

Sheldon, the H-37, and the HUIA, which had been (mostly) repaired, headed back up onto the mountain in the morning. The H-37 flew to the Kahiltna Glacier, where it intended to land at about sixty-five hundred feet. Denali was not exactly cooperative; a flare tossed from the copter to determine wind direction was blown back into the aircraft, "but was extinguished after a fearful minute." The maximum altitude for the smaller chopper was 17,400 feet, but it was still unable to land where Day and the Whittakers were holed up. Rescuers from Seattle, shuttled by air to Summit, were flown onto the Kahiltna by a short list of bush pilots from Talkeetna recruited by Sheldon. A base camp of operations was set up at 10,200 feet. Rescuers who'd been deposited lower on the Kahiltna began climbing to the base camp, while others from the base camp ascended toward 14,300 feet to establish a higher camp.

Higher on the mountain, a rescue toboggan, called an akja, was air-dropped to the Anchorage camp, where Bading continued to fail. Paul Crews and Charles Metzger loaded the sick woman into the sled and began to lower her down the mountain, tethered to a rope left by a Japanese summit team. Johnston was airlifted to help with the descent, and when Bading finally reached the camp at 14,300, Sheldon flew her off the mountain to Talkeetna. She made a complete recovery: On May 23, a local newspaper reported she was tan and "appeared in excellent health." That had not been the case a few days prior, when HACE prompted Wilson's urgent call for her evacuation; descent again proved the best cure for the condition. "Normally your system adjusts as you go up the mountain," explained Bading, an experienced mountaineer who had summited peaks in Alaska's Chugach and Aleutian ranges. "A tremendous headache was driving me nuts. Dr. Wilson said I was unconscious for a while. . . .

"Next time I'll do better," the climber declared.

While Bading was being rescued, pilot Link Luckett flew his Hiller 2E helicopter to the camp at 17,000 feet, "to make an estimate of the situation." That estimate in hand, he retreated to 14,300 feet, offloaded whatever he deemed unnecessary from his craft to make it lighter—seat cushions, extra fuel, a door, and the battery once the copter was started—and flew to the high camp again. "A spectacular landing at 17,000 feet allowed John Day to be snatched from the mountain," Johnston wrote. Luckett described the landing, on a blue ice field covered in new-fallen snow, this way: "Let's say it [was] just like landing on a big meringue pie."

As climbers converged on the camp at 14,300 feet, pilots continued to drop supplies. Not all the flyers were successful, however. Aviator William Stevenson, a volunteer from Anchorage, and his spotter, Sergeant Robert Elliott, a paramedic stationed at Elmendorf, were authorized to make a drop at the 14,300-foot camp but decided to fly higher, hoping to reach the 17,000-foot camp. The Cessna 180 didn't make it, crashing and burning at the top of the West Buttress.

The plane "made a couple of passes and crashed into the ice in a vertical dive," Jim Whittaker recalled. "This was a shock to us. . . . It was the low point of the trip. We couldn't get close enough to the plane and just stood helpless. They must have been killed instantly." The pilot and his passenger remain buried in Denali's ice; in accounts of the rescue, their loss seems minimized, a tragic side note in the drama of the rescue. But resources were precious, and the focus had to remain on the living.

The following day, May 21, Luckett continued his successful rescues at 17,000 feet, picking up the struggling Pete Schoening. Camps on the mountain were consolidating, and climbers were being airlifted off the peak as the weather was expected to take a turn for the worse. Rainier climber Dee Molenaar and two others made the long ascent to the highest camp, where the Whittaker twins remained hunkered down; the three Washington-based mountaineers began the descent while the others disassembled the camp. They stopped at the camp at 14,300 feet, rested and hydrated, then continued down to a supply camp at 13,200 feet. The men who broke down the high camp also descended to 14,300 feet, hauling packs that weighed as much as ninety pounds.

Overnight, Denali whipped up a storm. At the supply camp, the Seattle climbers huddled in a single tent, anchoring it with their bodies, after winds in excess of a hundred miles per hour blew the smaller tents away. By the morning of May 23, up to three feet of new snow had been dumped. Knowing they'd never make it down without snowshoes, the climbers still at 14,300 feet stamped a request for the necessary gear into the powder, hoping a plane would fly over. Radio contact was spotty. And the weather remained fitful. When the cloud cover lifted a bit, the climbers at 13,200 feet made the choice to bail out while they could, retreating to the base camp. Lou and Jim Whittaker, the last of the beleaguered Day expedition, were evacuated from there by air.

Weather windows opened on May 24 and 25, allowing flyers to take to the air for supply drops. Sheldon was a "welcome sight" at 14,300 feet, offloading snowshoes to those men so they could continue down the hill. By May 26 cloud cover again stymied evacuations: "Time after time the weather ship would go up and radio back a negative report," Johnston wrote. But finally, a break permitted the last of the rescuers to be airlifted off the mountain and down to Anchorage: "The curtain was rung down on the largest scale mountain rescue operation ever accomplished in North America."

Though Day had something else in mind, his rescue, and that of Helga Bading, ended up setting lasting records on the peak. Longtime Denali mountaineering ranger Roger Robinson, thinking back on the events that followed the fall, believes it was the most expensive rescue ever conducted on the mountain. Resources poured into the park from throughout Alaska and beyond, especially from the Pacific Northwest, where climbers were galvanized by the plight of their friends and colleagues, the Whittakers.

For Robinson, a student of aviation firsts on Denali, it's not just the rescue effort that sets the Day story apart. The flights of Don Sheldon in his Super Cub and the other flyers in their fixed-wing airships represented the first time supplies were dropped at those altitudes. The airlifts of Bading and Day, along with supply runs for the stranded climbers and rescuers, represented the first time helicopters were flown to an altitude of seventeen thousand feet.

"We tried real hard to make this a good expedition, and I am sorry we created so much trouble," Day wrote in the letter to park superintendent Samuel King that accompanied his accident report. "Our appreciation to your organization, and to the others who helped in the rescue is very great—and difficult to express properly." The Whittakers, Schoening, and Bading all voiced similar sentiments; no one doubted something extraordinary had occurred on the mountain in those long days of May.

While Day's mountaineering star faded following his Denali expedition, the Whittakers' stars ascended. They continued to push the limits on Everest, on Rainier, and on other peaks. They created and nurtured iconic businesses in the outdoor recreation industry: Jim founded Recreational Equipment Inc., better known as REI, and Lou founded Rainier Mountaineering Inc. (RMI), a guide service focused on the namesake volcano and other mountaineering destinations. Their time on Denali in 1960, as summiters, guides, rescuers, and the rescued, is a single chapter in a volume encompassing decades of high adventure.

The Third Time's a Charm

For a time, climbers from Korea were a nightmare on Denali. The lure of the mountain was irresistible to unprepared Asian climbers who proved not only a hazard to themselves, but also to those who had to rescue them. Through the 1980s and into the early 1990s the park's mountaineering summaries are riddled with reports of injured Korean alpinists and dead Korean alpinists. Park service correspondence from 1992 notes 10 percent of Korean climbers required rescue over the previous few years, a rate "100 times higher than for American climbers and significantly higher than for any other country with a similar number of climbers!"

The problem was threefold, rangers from Denali informed the Korean Alpine Federation. Two of the issues—Denali's relative proximity to Korea, making it an easy world-class pick, and the Korean inclination to "place reaching the summit above all else, including the loss of life and limb"— were considered geographical and cultural facts of life, components of the life-and-death problem that park officials, including climbing rangers, couldn't change. The third, the "misconception that Mt. McKinley [as the peak was then known] is a good training climb for higher peaks in the world," was an idea that could be disabused.

"Mt. McKinley is one of the coldest and most extreme mountains on this planet," ranger J. D. Swed warned aspiring Korean alpinists. "Every person planning an expedition here must physically and mentally be prepared for these conditions and be prepared not to reach the summit but return home with the satisfaction of coming away with life and limb."

Of the many rescues of Korean teams in those years, one stands out. In June 1986 a seven-man expedition arrived on the mountain. The plan: Two

The summit ridges of Denali and surrounding peaks are blanketed in fresh snow.
NATIONAL PARK SERVICE. PHOTO: DAVE WEBER

separate pairs of climbers from the team would make summit attempts via the Cassin Ridge, one of the more formidable routes on Denali, while the rest of the team remained lower on the mountain in support. Two climbers, Lee Jung Kwan and Chung Seoung Kwon, both in their late twenties, moved up the ridge at a fast clip, establishing four camps in four days, the highest at 6,050 meters, or about 19,800 feet.

But Kwan developed a headache at the team's 16,600-foot camp, and by the time he reached the high camp, altitude sickness was in full bloom. The climber was in serious enough trouble for the partners to radio their support camp for help. They were advised by their teammates to rest for a day, with the expectation that time would allow Kwan to better acclimate. Unfortunately, that's not always the way it works. To reverse the potentially deadly symptoms of high-altitude pulmonary edema (an accumulation of fluid in the lungs that obstructs breathing) or high-altitude cerebral edema (an accumulation of fluid that causes the brain to swell), climbers must descend. As Denali ranger Scott Gill observes in the *American Alpine Journal* report on the incident, at high altitudes on Denali "one is constantly deteriorating, and can never regain full strength." The sick climber had to come down to get better.

That didn't happen. Instead, six days after arriving on the mountain, the two men tried for the summit. But Kwan was suffering from ataxia, a lack of coordination symptomatic of cerebral edema, and the climbers were forced to abandon the attempt and return to their high camp.

There, things got even more critical: Their stove quit, and they ran out of food. The men had carried six days' worth of supplies onto the mountain, traveling light and moving quickly with the hope of avoiding any turn in the weather. Now they had no way to boil water, and no way to replace the calories they were burning just to stay warm and alive. Theirs was a shitstorm of their own making.

Heading down was the most logical response as hardships accumulated, but retreat was problematic, given Kwan's weakening condition, the difficulty of the terrain, and the fact that the team's fifty-meter rope—the only rope they carried—was insufficient for the task of rappelling to safety from their bivouac.

Even as the situation worsened, with plunging temperatures, increasing wind speeds, and accumulating snowfall adding layers of complication, the healthier climber, Kwon, made another pair of attempts on the summit. He gained a hundred meters on the first try; the second time, he realized he was too weak to continue, and down-climbed to camp, where his partner continued to suffer.

For a time, mountaineering rangers monitoring the situation hoped the second Korean summit team from the expedition, composed of three climbers, would be able to assist the higher pair. But they had problems of their own, having lost a pack containing critical gear, including a stove and sleeping bag, when they clipped it into a fixed line that failed. That team eventually retreated, leaving their countrymen stranded above.

On June 19, six days after they set off on their summit bid, the Koreans in the high camp began relaying an SOS via radio. It was picked up in Talkeetna by mountaineering rangers, including Roger Robinson, but exactly what the two climbers needed was not clear. The language barrier proved confounding. Because no one was sure what was being said, and just how dire the situation might be, recordings of the transmissions were relayed to the Korean consulate in Anchorage for translation. There another problem was identified: The climbers were attempting to communicate in English, so the Koreans couldn't understand them either.

Rangers turned to Talkeetna pilot Lowell Thomas for assistance. Thomas and an interpreter, Mr. Park, flew up toward the stranded climbers, but were forced back by weather before they could make radio or visual contact. Upon his return to Talkeetna, however, Mr. Park assured rangers the stranded climbers were, indeed, in distress.

While Mr. Park and the Korean base-camp team rendezvoused on the Kahiltna Glacier, rangers assembled a search-and-rescue team in Talkeetna. The first thought Robinson, ranger Gill, and their cohorts had was to enlist the assistance of a British team that was completely acclimated, having just summited and returned safely to the little drinking town with a climbing problem. The team told the rangers they'd be ready to rumble in the morning, and headed off to the bar at the Fairview Inn to celebrate their accomplishment. They could handle their alcohol, they assured Robinson.

Come time for departure early the next morning, however, none of the Brits were fit to climb. The party had been too hearty, the hangovers were too profound, and the rangers were forced to come up with plan B.

Fortunately there were options. Robinson and his colleagues rallied back at the ranger station and cobbled together a different SAR team. Australian Gary Scott was the volunteer manager of the medical/rescue camp at 14,200 feet on the Kahiltna; he'd been there for five weeks, knew the mountain, and was acclimated. Austrians Wolfgang Wippler and Arthur Horied had just successfully completed a traverse of Denali (going up one side and down the other), and though they'd only slept for a couple of hours, were on board for the mission. So were volunteers Peter Downing and Vern Tejas, a guide with the service run by legendary Denali summiter and guide Ray Genet. Tejas, a formidable climber who would complete ascents of the Seven Summits, the highest points on each continent, not once, but ten times, had just topped out on Denali and was not hung over.

The Kahiltna Glacier serves as the starting point for most mountaineers on Denali, including climber Vern Tejas, who tapped the highest points on the mountain three times in short order. DENALI NATIONAL PARK AND PRESERVE MUSEUM COLLECTIONS. PHOTO: BOB BUTTS

Three members of the rescue party were airlifted from Talkeetna to the Kahiltna base camp at 7,000 feet, where Tejas and Downing were picked up. The Bell 212, piloted by Ron Smith, then flew up to the medical rescue camp at 14,200 feet, where it deposited everyone but Tejas and Scott, who stayed on board to help drop a cache of supplies for the SAR higher on the West Buttress route. Weather on the peak was deteriorating, however, so after the drop, the Bell 212 flew the two climbers back to the 14,200-foot camp and retreated to Talkeetna.

In the medical/rescue camp, the team assessed the situation faced by the Koreans, conditions on the mountain, and the capabilities of the climbers attempting the rescue. The decision was to send Scott, Wippler, and Tejas over the summit and down to the distressed climbers; the three men then would lead the Koreans back over the top onto the West Buttress route and down to an elevation where they could be airlifted out. Meanwhile, Downing and Horied, who was suffering from altitude sickness, as well as ranger Ralph Moore and a group of volunteers, would ferry supplies from the 14,200-foot camp to higher camps in support of the advance team.

Tejas, Wippler, and Scott began the ascent. They were acclimated all right, but they were also beat. Regardless of a climber's level of fitness, the combination of altitude, temperature, physical exertion, and amount of time spent on Denali takes its toll. Scott felt weak and unsteady as the team approached 17,300 feet, where they picked up oxygen and a two-hundred-meter rescue rope, adding considerable weight to their loads. Before the team reached the top of the fixed lines, the Aussie had to back off, compromised by the altitude and exhaustion. "Gary was acclimatized, but had been off the mountain [for a time]," Tejas recalled. "And then half of the air was taken away."

At Denali Pass, at 18,300 feet, Wippler and Tejas encountered the camp of another ascent team, led by guides Tejas knew. Wippler, who'd done the traverse, was also spent, and needed to rest. He told Tejas he just needed an hour to sleep, and he crawled into a tent, out of the weather, for a quick reboot. Tejas was still in good shape, able to keep climbing, so the Austrian told him to carry on, and to count on him meeting Tejas on the summit to assist.

Tejas's decision to continue the mission on his own was not without conflict. He had a reputation as a maverick, and now he demonstrated how he'd earned it. Rangers in Talkeetna very clearly, and very wisely, voiced their concerns about a one-man rescue effort, he recalled, admitting, "That's not a good ratio for a rescue."

But Tejas was already invested in the endeavor, having climbed for six hours and attained a vertical mile. He told the rangers he was going on, if only to look over the ridge and assess the possibilities. Then he faked radio trouble, telling them that he needed to save batteries and he'd get back to them. "I didn't listen to them. I was strong, I was motivated, and theoretically two people's lives were on the line."

Tejas was determined not to let the Korean victim die on the mountain. He also had a deeply personal motivation for getting onto the high ground alone; he'd lost his girlfriend a year earlier, and had brought her ashes to the summit the previous year. As he climbed, he had a lot of time to think about Marilee, how much she meant to him and how fragile life was. "I got quite emotional, crying on and off, tears freezing in my beard. [But] I definitely wanted to help the Koreans out. I kept on going, tears coming down, [with] mixed emotions." He wanted to be alone with her, there on the mountain, but he had a job to do.

Tejas lugged the heavy rope, pickets to create anchors, some lunch, and the radio to the summit area, tapping it for the second time. When he reached the top of the Cassin Ridge, however, he realized he really had no practical way to determine where the distressed climbers were. The musician in Tejas had a solution. He was a "hot-shot yodeler," and he knew most climbers associated yodeling with alpine mountain guides— it's an international mountain signal. He called out from the high ridge, then listened for a response . . . and got one.

"Holy smokes," he thought. "Somebody's alive down there."

Once he heard an answer from the Koreans, Tejas anchored his line and descended toward the trapped team, dropping six hundred feet—the length of the rope—to where he hoped the men were bivouacked. Nobody was there. He'd reached the end of his rappel, but the Koreans were fifty feet down the Cassin.

Tejas was undeterred. He down-climbed from the end of the rope—his protection—to the small tent where the afflicted climber and his partner were sheltering. "It wasn't too steep," he said.

Tejas found the two "awake, oriented, hungry, and very thirsty," though Kwan was desperately ill. The rescuer gave the man dexamethasone (Decadron), a powerful steroid commonly used by mountaineers to temporarily stave off mountain sickness. Then he gave some to the other climber and took some himself. All three, Tejas recalled, felt better after taking the medication, his "go-to emergency drug." The food, the water, the drug, "and a live body outside saying let's go was enough to rally spirits," Tejas said.

As incapacitated as he was, Kwan retained some of his climbing abilities. He tied into the rope, and "that was a good idea but totally inadequate as there was no one above to pull him up," Tejas recalled. The only way to get him the medical help he needed, Tejas knew, was to go back over the top. His third time on Denali's summit slopes in the span of days would prove the charm that saved the stricken climber's life.

In Robinson's words, Tejas essentially pushed the afflicted Korean climber to the top, while the healthier Kwon followed, hauling a pack of supplies. They ascended side by side, Kwan on the rope and Tejas free-climbing. The guide had done the route before, in the 1980s, and knew the upper part was steep, but not so steep he could slip and die. Tejas breathed with the sick man, coaxed him to slide one ascender up the rope, then the other, and when Kwan grew weaker, moved the ascenders for him. "We ratcheted him up with verbal reinforcement and encouragement," the climber explained.

That effort, in Robinson's experience, represents "the greatest rescue that has ever occurred on Denali to date. Nothing else is in the caliber."

When the climbers finally got over the summit ridge, Kwan slipped into a coma. Both Koreans, Tejas remembered, were "working under the misconception there was a group at the top to take them away." When the sick man arrived on the summit slopes and looked around, he saw no one. Wippler would make good on his promise to meet Tejas on the summit, carrying the rescue sled and oxygen, about ten minutes later. But Kwan was done; he'd used all his energy to climb those six hundred feet. He laid down on the slope and didn't get up.

Once Wippler was on the scene, the two rescuers administered oxygen with hopes of reviving the ailing climber. It didn't really work, so Tejas and Wippler loaded him into a sled and began to lower him down the mountain, slowly and carefully, six hundred feet at a time.

Elsewhere on the mountain and in the air, other elements of the SAR effort were mobilized. Pilot Thomas flew his plane overhead, hoping to drop supplies to the team, but given the sketchy weather the rescuers on the ground determined it was better to just keep heading downhill. When they reached the camp of the expedition near Denali Pass, they left the Koreans in the care of those climbers and descended to high camp, where Tejas crawled into an igloo and slept.

Rescuers spent one more day on the descent with the two Koreans, engaged in "difficult lowering and hauling," to reach 17,300 feet, where Kwan was airlifted off the mountain. Kwon made it to the high camp a hundred feet lower, then he, too, was flown to a hospital. But before he left, the Korean climber gave Tejas twenty dollars. "It is from the bottom of my heart," Kwon told the rescuer. "Would you please accept it?"

Tejas did, recognizing the symbolism. The gift-giving was important for Kwon. But for Tejas, acknowledgment of his efforts wasn't, and isn't, what mattered.

"I was motivated; I was a volunteer; we put our bodies in dangerous places to help people in danger," Tejas told me, the spirit of SAR voiced in both word and tone. The people working search and rescue are good, capable, modest, and hardworking, in his estimation. He's honored to have had a ranger like Robinson praise the incredible effort that went into the Korean rescue, but said, "however, that's not why we do it."

And in this instance, Tejas's grief yielded to his willpower and motivation. He was "emotionally wrung out" as he made the solo trek toward the top of the Cassin. He'd been powerless to save his girlfriend's life, but in that moment, despite feeling fragile, he carried on. "We can do significant things," he said, "despite feeling powerless."

After the rescue, Tejas continued his remarkable and storied mountaineering career. His résumé includes those multiple ascents of the coveted Seven Summits, as well as the first solo winter ascent of Denali in 1988.

And the adventure is ongoing. For this mountaineer, four times, ten times, as many times as possible, or as necessary, is the charm.

A Man on a String:
The Thunder Mountain Rescue

————————

Thunder Mountain was a warm-up climb for two experienced climbers from Boulder, Colorado. Malcolm Daly and Jim Donini intended to spend a few days tackling a new route up the south face of the peak before making an attempt on the higher, more challenging Mount Hunter, their ultimate goal.

The trip was Daly's maiden foray into Alaskan mountaineering, and it proved as challenging and spectacular as he'd anticipated. The forty-three-year-old climber was encountering terrain and isolation like no other in his experience. That isolation was made more complete by the fact that Donini, an experienced Alaskan mountaineer, opted not to carry a radio. Once pilot Paul Roderick deposited the two men on the Tokositna Glacier, a long arm of ice stretching fingers to the base of the summits that make up the Hunter massif, the two men had no way to communicate with the outside world, much less summon a rescue.

The team attempted to ascend the twenty-five-hundred-foot-long line, comprised of snowfields, steps of rock and ice, and a final ribbon of ice in a couloir, a couple of times before the accident occurred. The first time they turned back because one of Donini's crampons failed. The second time, Daly got pinged by a chunk of ice; they retreated with the intent to return once the functionality of his arm wasn't compromised.

On the third attempt, the climbers made good progress, ascending the varied terrain with confidence in good weather. Daly was in the lead as they approached the top of the ice ribbon ... and then a block of ice careened down the chute; an ice screw failed. It all went bad. The mountaineer peeled free, and the fall propelled him nearly two hundred feet down the narrow corridor. On the way down he collided with Donini, impaling his partner's thigh with the twelve points of his crampons. Donini was able to arrest Daly's fall, but the damage was done.

In conversation on the *Sharp End*, an American Alpine Club podcast, Daly admits he doesn't remember exactly what happened. According to the accident reports, he sustained blows to his head that initially rendered him unconscious, and then woozy. He also suffered a compound fracture of one leg and shattered the other ankle. But from reserves in his unconscious, he was able to secure himself to the mountain with an anchor, which enabled Donini to rappel down and assess the damage.

The older climber did what he could to stabilize the injured man. Working with a first-aid kit that contained "a roll of tape, a bandanna, and a Swiss Army knife," and perched on a narrow shelf he'd chipped into the ice, Donini bound Daly's legs together, using an ice ax for a splint, and worked to prevent shock from setting in. He lowered Daly two hundred feet down the steep ice slope, then realized he'd be unable to complete the task on his own and that, given his injuries, Daly wasn't likely to survive the trauma a descent would inflict. The two men decided the best option—really the only option—was for Donini to proceed down solo and go for help.

Donini made sure his partner was securely anchored on a ledge that, again, he chipped into the mountainside. He also made sure Daly had the supplies—extra clothing, food, water—he'd need to survive. He left his pack, too, so Daly had something to sit on. Then, belayed by Daly, Donini down-climbed the chute and out onto the glacier below.

The separation of the partnership is something Daly lingers on in his recollection of the climb, noting that it was a "big deal" when he finally had to let the rope go and watched it slither down the face to Donini, out of sight. But the partners had talked it through, and the decision to separate was right.

"If we'd had a backpack full of first aid equipment and SAM splints and stuff we probably could have self-rescued, but we didn't," he told Ashley

Saupe, a fellow mountaineer and the podcast host. "I gave [Jim] a pat on the back metaphorically and said, 'Man, go for it. My life is in your hands.'"

As luck would have it, Donini reached the glacier at the same time pilot Roderick was flying over, checking on the climbers he'd dropped there days before. Daly believes the flyer's "Spidey sense"—the feeling that something was amiss—prompted the check-in. Donini flagged him down, Roderick landed and picked him up, and the two sped back to Talkeetna. Denali's mountaineering rangers, including Daryl Miller, who had climbed with Daly in Colorado, were waiting. The rescue operation was underway.

Despite uncooperative weather and a forecast predicting it would only get worse, three rangers climbed aboard a helicopter piloted by Jim Hood and flew out to survey the site of Daly's hanging bivouac. The intent was to scope the possibilities for a short haul—a procedure that involves lowering a rescuer and a basket or harness on a line suspended from a helicopter to an otherwise inaccessible accident site, securing the injured to that line, and then reeling both rescuer and rescued to safety.

Rangers prepare a short-haul rescue by, as captioned by the National Park Service, taking the helo for a walk.
NATIONAL PARK SERVICE PHOTO

In this instance, however, the short haul would require Denali's special-ized high-altitude Lama helicopter to hover dangerously close to cliff walls in uncertain winds. Hood determined it was too tight, too dangerous. The plan was nixed.

The rangers then considered the situation from a grounded perspec-tive. Could they reach Daly by descending from the top down? Or climb-ing from the bottom up? Given the geography of the mountainside and the meteorology buffeting it, neither option was more promising than the short haul. The dangers of rock and icefall creaming a rescuer ascending the chute, or rocketing down onto Daly as rescuers descended from above, were too substantial.

Meanwhile, reinforcements were mobilizing, including the Alaska High Mountain Rescue Team and the 210th Pararescue Squad. And there was another helicopter pilot in the mix who offered a different haul option, according to Miller. Karl Cotton, on contract with an air-taxi service in Talkeetna, was recognized as one of the best long-line pilots in the world. Could Cotton, using the Lama and his prodigious long-haul skills, pluck Daly safely off the wall?

The park service's incident commander thought no. Despite his experi-ence, the Los Angeles–based pilot had never flown in Alaska. For the time being, the long haul was off the table.

Night descended. On Thunder Mountain, avalanches of spindrift, gauzy and gentle as avalanches go, rained down on Daly, anchored alone on the ice. The injured man took stock of his rations, did what he could to ease his own pain, and survived.

The next day, the full force of Denali's SAR machine deployed on the glacier, determined to pluck Daly safely and quickly from his perch. Para-jumpers, delivered in a Pave Hawk helicopter, were there; Denali's climb-ing rangers were there; volunteers from Alaska Mountain Rescue Group were there. Daly recalls waking up to a layer of clouds, like "cotton batting," blanketing the mountain and a fixed-wing aircraft appearing in a hole in the fluff, acknowledging him with a dip of a wing. The weather was also permissive enough to allow a helicopter to land on the snowfield above where the injured man was anchored, but the concussion of the rotors triggered an avalanche. While Daly feared being clobbered by the full force of the slab, the terrain was so steep it mostly washed past him; it was like being behind a waterfall, he told Saupe.

On the rescue side, the ground-based options were reviewed again, and again. With Miller using his prodigious experience to guide the decision-making, he maintained that climbing up to Daly, or climbing down to him, was too hazardous. The parajumpers and volunteers steamed with frustration.

Another night settled over the camp on the glacier. Another night settled over Daly on the mountainside. He did exactly what he needed do: He decided to live. The solitary man passed the time with a "counting game," spinning his arms like windmills, doing crunches over and over again, and thinking of his wife and children. He survived.

The next morning dawned clear, and Miller activated the crews on the glacier, getting them geared up. He also was willing to allow Cotton, the ace pilot from Los Angeles, to take a look at the situation.

What would you need to make a short haul off Thunder Mountain work? Miller asked the flyer.

I'd need a two-hundred-foot rope, and I could hover there all day, Cotton replied.

The maneuvers that ensued, as described by Miller, are mind-boggling. The rangers rigged a line to the proper length and attached a GOD ring—a big steel O-ring integral for attaching control lines, baskets, and pulleys in a rescue. Rangers Billy Shott, Meg Perdue, and Miller loaded into the Lama, with Cotton at the controls. Shott, the ranger corps's "wild man," was at the sharp end of the rope with the basket. Perdue was the spotter: She called off the distances to the ground for the ranger on the rope, and from the helicopter's rotor blades to the cliff walls for the pilot. She also watched the weather. Miller was in charge.

The Lama, guided by Cotton, rose into position, and Shott descended toward the mountainside. Just as the ranger got to the two-hundred-foot mark, clouds rolled in and Cotton was forced to pull away.

On the second attempt the pilot set the ranger down about seventy-five feet below the climber. Shott ascended to Daly, clipped him in, and then, with a "big pendulum swing out," Cotton lifted rescuer and rescued free and away.

It was like watching a man twenty feet up a ladder drop a string into a bowl, Miller recalled. And it was a good ending, given that without the risky maneuver, Daly's bones might still be hanging in the chute. Though Daly suffered frostbite in addition to his other injuries, and would eventually lose a foot, he has gone on to lead a full and active life, including creating the nonprofit Paradox Sports, which enables folks with disabilities to do what he had done: explore their remodeled physical potential as climbers and mountaineers.

Reflecting on the rescue, Miller recalled receiving a message from Daly in the Talkeetna station prior to his arrival in the park: "Your worst nightmare is coming." That turned out to be true. As incident commander for Daly's rescue, Miller had faced one of the trickiest aspects of that position. He was a friend of the victim's, and the last thing he wanted to do—the last thing he ever wanted to do, in any rescue—was leave a friend to die on a mountain. The other last thing he ever wanted to do, in any rescue, was lose a rescuer. Every decision he made factored in this calculus. Daly was where he was, and he'd put himself there with no expectation of rescue. The rescuers—parajumpers, volunteers, rangers—were there to help if they could, but also to live to help another day. In the end, it all worked, for Daly, for the rescuers, and for Miller.

For his part, his connections with Miller, with Billy Shott (another friend), with Jim Donini, and with others in the climbing community were crucial to his survival, Daly told Saupe in his podcast interview. Those connections engendered a level of trust and confidence that tethered him to life, and were maintained even after the letting-go, the powerful moment when Daly dropped the rope to Donini on the descent, severing the physical link. "The rope is such a powerful symbol of the partnership," he said.

But even when the string that connected him slipped out of sight, it remained, hitching him to the mountain and to the people he loved.

I Need a Diet Coke

He tried a couple of times in those early July days of 1991, but couldn't quite claim Denali's summit. On his final attempt, the mountain stopped Krzysztof Wiecha about five hundred vertical feet short of the South Peak. And things got complicated.

Wiecha first attempted the summit on July 3 with a partner; the two reached the seventeen-thousand-foot level but conditions didn't allow them to climb higher. The next day, the Fourth of July, a team guided by Rainier Mountaineering Inc. launched an assault, and Wiecha tagged along. When the High One countered with worsening weather the RMI team abandoned its bid, turned back, and safely descended.

But Wiecha was not dissuaded and pushed on, traveling light to travel fast, outfitted with only a rucksack, a canteen, a snack, and an ice ax. He made it to about 19,800 feet before wind and cold shut down all human progress on the summit ridges. The climber disappeared into Denali's infamous howl.

"We thought he was a dead man," Denali mountaineering ranger Daryl Miller recalled. "The winds were nuking things up there."

On his own and with no hope of descent until the storm abated, the twenty-eight-year-old mountaineer sought shelter in a crevasse and dug in. To keep warm he kept digging. For three days he dug, and dug, and dug, wandering from place to place around the mountaintop while the weather raged. He carried no sleeping bag, bivouac, or tent; he had no fuel or stove to melt snow for water. Armed with stamina, an ice ax, and an incredible will to live, Wiecha fended off hypothermia, dehydration, exhaustion, and despair.

Rangers and the park service geologist program a weather station atop Kahiltna Pass. The stations, installed in 2019, keep tabs on the winds and storms that regularly rake the peak. NATIONAL PARK SERVICE. PHOTO: PETER HAEUSSLER

"Sometimes I was cold," the climber told a reporter from his hospital bed in the days following his rescue. "I ate snow and tried to keep busy making snow shelters, but I forgot about my feet." Wiecha may have forgotten about them because they were completely numb, the cold working through boot and fiber to flesh and bone, freezing cells deemed expendable by Wiecha's body as it shunted blood and the warmth it contained to his core and his brain. Heart and mind were indispensable; toes could go.

On July 6, when the winds abated enough to allow reconnaissance by air, a Talkeetna pilot flew a Cessna 206 around the summit in what rangers assumed would become a search for a body. But Wiecha heard the engine's call and made his appearance, "waving out of a crack" in the snow. Amazed and relieved, rescuers put together a survival kit—hot cocoa, food, a sleeping bag—to tide the climber over until they could reach him. But the air-drop didn't go as planned and the goods rolled away, out of reach of the stranded and crippled man.

Fortunately, while a packet dropped from a fixed-wing aircraft was an excellent option given the circumstances, it wasn't the only tool in the park service's SAR kit. In the summer of 1991 Denali National Park and Preserve made a significant addition to its rescue arsenal: a state-of-the-art Aerospatiale Lama high-altitude rescue helicopter. The Lama—light, nimble, and powerful—was designed to change out patrols at eighteen thousand feet in the towering ranges of India and Nepal, and was on call to replace the US Army Chinook helicopters typically flown on Alaskan rescue missions. The new craft now had a chance to prove its mettle on the highest mountain in North America.

Miller and fellow Denali ranger Jim Phillips climbed aboard the airship and were flown to Denali's "Football Field," a large, relatively gentle slope at about 19,500 feet, below the summit ridge. From there they ascended on foot to where Wiecha was hunkered down.

"We asked how he was doing," Miller remembers. The climber said he was OK. He also wanted a Diet Coke.

Of course, OK was a relative term, given the situation. Wiecha's feet were badly frostbitten, and he was in no condition to make a descent. The rangers employed "pendulum lowerings" to drop the climber onto the Football Field, and the Lama lifted him off the mountain from there and carried him safely away.

Miller and Phillips were not so lucky; the Lama's weight limits precluded their evacuation from the Heights at the same time as Wiecha. While they waited for the Lama to return, Denali got grumpy, whipping up conditions that prohibited another landing. The rangers were forced to make their own way down from the heights. Miller, having been deposited at 19,500 feet without acclimating, suffered the headache, nausea, and other discomforts of acute mountain sickness. And travel on the mountain was sketchy—slopes were icy, visibility was limited, winds were brutal. The two men feared for their lives as they negotiated the Autobahn, a steep slope linking Denali Pass, at 18,200 feet, to the high camp at 17,200 feet. As mentioned previously, a slip on the Autobahn can—and has—resulted in an accelerating race into injury or oblivion. Slowly and carefully, the men down-climbed to the safety of the lower camps, then off the mountain.

In the aftermath of the rescue, Miller and Wiecha became friends. The climber's adventure took a significant toll: His feet were so badly frostbitten they couldn't be saved and were amputated in the hospital in Anchorage. But that trauma didn't dampen Wiecha's spirit, which had proven indomitable in the days he spent digging dollops of warmth nearly four miles high in a frozen hurricane. The resilient Pole was outfitted with state-of-the-art prosthetics, and worked to pay off his hospital bills, solidifying Miller's respect. Wiecha also continued to aspire to Denali's summit, reportedly returning to Talkeetna to train for another attempt (though I couldn't confirm he ever followed through), and also became a Polish ambassador to the Special Olympics in Alaska, according to Miller.

Wiecha's rescue also established a baseline for what Denali's search-and-rescue teams could do on the mountain with the Lama. After the rescue, rangers started pushing the limits of high-altitude flight—no surprise given the nature of the park and the people who work there. Over the summer of 1991 the Lama was used in five rescues, including two above 18,000 feet and the one at the 19,500-foot-high Football Field. In 1992 the Lama was employed in short-haul rescues: Rangers clipped into fixed lines dropped from the helicopter's belly and were deposited in places where the airship couldn't land; the climbers in trouble clipped into the same lines and were hoisted into the craft for evacuation. In 1993 the Lama landed on the summit, at 20,310 feet. In the years that have followed, the Lama has proven its worth over and over again, a frequent flyer to the high ground, referenced repeatedly in the park's mountaineering records, used by ranger pilots to carry away climbers suffering the devastating effects of altitude, those injured in slides and avalanches, those hailing from hometowns around the globe, those seeking records of every imaginable kind, those trapped by Denali's notorious weather, even those who've pocked the mountaintop with snow caves and have come away with a craving for Diet Coke.

For Want of a Chisel:
The Art and Science of Crevasse Rescue

Crevasses do not have silver linings. Those who've fallen in and lived to tell the tale unanimously agree: A crevasse is a place to exit as quickly as possible. There's absolutely no reason to linger.

More often than not, those who tumble in are able to climb out, either on their own or with help from fellow climbers. But falls and recoveries are not without tension.

In 1932 Denali's chief ranger, Grant Pearson, experienced firsthand the wicked trap of the crevasse. He was no stranger to glacier travel on the mountain; in fact, he'd been immersed in it since his arrival in the fledgling Mount McKinley National Park in the mid-1920s. Still, in his *My Life of High Adventure*, this man of great humor is deadly serious when he describes his time in "that deadly cold-storage locker."

Pearson was part of the four-man Lindley-Liek expedition, the second team to reach the summit. His journey was the best of times and the worst, a challenge on a variety of levels for a man in love with Denali and destined to be one of the park's greatest superintendents. A sampling of his native optimism and fearlessness: He embarked on the expedition, which sought to reach the summit on skis ... with no experience on skis. Another team member, who happened to be an expert telemarker, did his best to instruct the neophyte, hoping to save him the embarrassment of looking like "a snowman on a bender," Pearson wrote. As for his opinion on skiing in general? "'These things,' I thought, falling over backwards, 'are just a fad.'"

On descent, after summiting both Denali's North and South Peaks (a first), Pearson was snowshoeing along behind his partners when the bottom dropped out. "I had time to let out a feeble shout," he recalled. "Then, for a couple of long, long seconds I plummeted downward. I remember thinking, 'This is it, fellow!' Then my pack scraped against the side of the crevasse, my head banged hard against the ice wall and I came to a jarring stop."

Forty feet above him, sunlight filtered through the hole where he'd punched through a snow bridge. Pearson estimated the crevasse gaped twelve feet wide at the surface; he was stuck on a plug of snow at a point where about two feet separated the ice walls. And "below was icy death."

The ranger's partners heard his cry and returned to his rescue. While he firmed up his position within the crevasse, sinking his crampons into the ice rather than trust his perch on the snow plug, Pearson's teammates lowered a rope. First they hauled up the pack, loaded with precious supplies. Next they tried to haul up Pearson. "I moved about six inches, and stopped," he wrote. "A hundred and eighty pounds of human was too much—not for the rope pullers but for the snow at the crevasse lip. The rope simply cut into the snow and caught in a bind."

But Pearson knew what to do. He told his partners to anchor themselves and the rope, and then raised himself out of the ice by climbing the lifeline hand over hand. Toward the top, the three on the surface "gave a hard pull. I flopped out on that open, blessed glacier-top like a fish yanked ashore." He emerged with minor injuries.

"I was lucky," he observed. He knew just how lucky: On the sled that had been pulled by his teammates just ahead was the body of Theodore Koven. He and one of his partners on the ill-fated Cosmic Ray expedition had perished on, and in, the same snowfield.

Denali National Park and Preserve encompasses hundreds of glaciers, so it makes sense Denali's mountaineering rangers are experts in the art and science of navigating them and conducting crevasse rescues. Like river runners read water, mountaineers read ice, cultivating a deep understanding of the shape-shifting nature of floes, of how they splinter and shatter as they slide over the rock formations below, of the forces that affect where crevasses open and close, and of when snow bridges form and melt away.

In the Northern Hemisphere, from Mount Rainier in Washington State to Mount Everest in the Himalaya, the optimal mountaineering season corresponds to weeks of predictably stable weather that can begin in late April and stretch into July. These windows making climbing possible, while at the same time heightening the dangers of crossing glaciers. Big mountains are also notorious for creating their own weather, which adds more uncertainty to the mix. On Denali, because of its northern latitude and extreme relief, weather creation takes on grander proportions and the climbing window brings with it a midnight sun, which accelerates melting of the snowpack. That, in turn, exposes more of each glacier's fractured, dynamic underpinnings. Plan a summit attempt too late in the season and snow bridges—their reliability a crapshoot anyway—are pretty much guaranteed to be compromised.

In the ideal scenario, when a mountaineer takes the plunge, a rope mate (maybe two, maybe more) remains successfully pinned to the top of the glacier in an arrest, ice ax and crampons jammed securely into packed snow on the upside. Companions set up a belay, then rig a rope system that'll enable them to hoist the fallen to safety. Words of encouragement filter down to the victim all the while. Teeth chattering with cold, nerves frayed, the climber in the crevasse does everything humanly possible to speed the escape.

Denali mountaineering ranger Daryl Miller's firsthand adventure within a crevasse mostly followed this script. It happened when he was tucked in the middle of an expedition traveling across the Muldrow Glacier as part of a National Outdoor Leadership School (NOLS) event. He was the man in the middle on a three-man rope team, and part of the third rope team ascending, when the bottom dropped out. Miller found himself neck deep in a crevasse others had safely traversed only moments before. His feet swung clear; there was nothing solid below. With both teammates, front and behind, in self-arrest, another rope team cautiously approached and threw Miller a rope. He, like Pearson, ended up safe on the blessed surface of the ice river.

The mental piece of the crevasse puzzle is critical. Preparation is key. Mountaineers should arrive on any glaciated peak as well schooled and proficient in the hows of safe travel as possible. They should also, ideally, set out across any booby-trapped ice field with the mindset that, as one alpinist put it, "You'll go in waist-deep, and it'll be an easy climb out."

But the fact is, on any glacier on any mountain any climber runs the risk of a horrible outcome. Those who emerge bring with them insights into the experiences of those who have disappeared forever into the void, where the bottomless darkness becomes real, and the reasons why rescue might not be possible are thrown into sharp, touchable focus. As it plays out, with all its "ifs" and complexities, the possibility of rescue becoming recovery moves front and center, along with the fact that even recovery may only be possible after a hundred-year-long ride to the toe of the impassive glacier. So many wildcards are at play on glaciated mountains in Alaska that what happens when a human slides between two blue walls—whether she just breaks the surface, lands unharmed on a ledge ten feet down, wedges like a chockstone in a slot, or vanishes into the black depths—is a stomach-churning unknown.

Read any tale of mountaineering on Denali and a crevasse fall—and subsequent rescue attempt—is likely part of the storyline. But slotting, because it occurs so rarely, sticks in the heads of mountaineering rangers. A pair of crevasse falls where the victim slotted in a crevasse, though separated by decades, miles, and technological advances, stand out in search-and-rescue annals on the mountain because they highlight both the best-case scenario and the worst, and show how time, innovation, and creativity have improved the odds for survival.

THE SLOT 1981

In early May 1981, Jim Wickwire and Chris Kerrebrock hatched a plan to ascend Denali via the Wickersham Wall. Located on the north side of the mountain, the fourteen-thousand-foot face is notorious for its incessant avalanches, icefalls, and impossibly steep terrain. It thwarted all attempts for decades, including the first, made in 1903 by the Alaskan political and frontier icon for whom the wall is named, Judge James Wickersham. Though the enticing, frightening face quashed his dreams of mountaineering glory, the one-time prospector earned other meritorious titles, becoming a territorial judge, founder of the school later called the University of Alaska, and champion of what would become Mount McKinley National Park. The mountaineers who finally did claim the first ascent of the wall, in 1963, hailed from the Harvard Mountaineering Club. The team took more than a month to scout and ascend the route, which had been scoped from the air by another Denali icon, Bradford Washburn.

The forty-year-old Wickwire and his twenty-five-year-old companion began their attempt on Denali with a traverse, hiking from the Kahiltna Glacier on the south side of the mountain over Kahiltna Pass to the Peters Glacier on the north. They descended the Peters Glacier toward the base of the Wickersham Wall on a beautiful day, threading through the small crevasses they were able to detect by subtle sags in the snowfields. Their sled, which they were both roped to, was unwieldy on the uneven surface, making passage down the ice field laborious. When the climbers finally encountered what appeared to be a smooth, gentle, clean slope leading to easier terrain along the glacier's lateral moraine, they headed that way.

Then, "without any warning whatsoever," Wickwire found himself "flying through the air ... and then, down." Kerrebrock had plunged into a hidden crevasse and Wickwire, along with the sled, hurtled in behind him.

"This is it," Wickwire thought, knowing from experience that the consequences of the fall were going to be "very, very serious."

The twenty-five-foot plunge ended with Kerrebrock wedged tightly in the narrowing crack, the heavy sled on top of him, and Wickwire on top of both, with a broken shoulder.

It was a bad scene, but both climbers were conscious, battling the urge to panic, and determined to meet the self-rescue challenge. Wickwire was no stranger to surviving extreme conditions on imposing peaks. He was part of the team that logged the first ascent of K2, arguably the most challenging peak in the Karakoram, and had been forced to bivouac overnight just below the summit, above twenty-seven thousand feet, without oxygen and with minimal protection. He survived hours alone in the "death zone." Kerrebrock was also an experienced mountaineer, a guide on the heavily crevassed Mount Rainier in Washington State. Helping themselves was their only option, and they reached into their physical and psychological toolboxes to make it happen.

The first move was Wickwire's. He knew the best way to free his wedged partner was by pulling him out from above, and that meant he had to get out of the crevasse. But the slot was so narrow he couldn't swing his ice ax or his feet to gain purchase. The alpinist spent the better part of an hour laboriously chipping tiny ledges in the ice wall to serve as platforms for the front points of his crampons.

Once atop the glacier, he fixed a picket, rigged an anchor, and began pulling on the rope, hoping to simply haul his partner out. When that failed, he lowered himself back into the crevasse to try something different. He used ascenders and his leg power to apply upward force, attempted to remove his partner's pack, chipped away at the ice walls; he did everything he knew to free Kerrebrock from the squeezing ice. It all failed. A terrible truth slowly became apparent to both men. The problem was unresolvable, and the cold was unrelenting. Wickwire, helpless and distraught, finally climbed back to the surface of the glacier and sat vigil on the edge of the crevasse as Kerrebrock, who'd passed from frustration and agitation at his predicament to a kind of acceptance, slowly succumbed to hypothermia. Before he died, he asked Wickwire to bring the mouthpiece of his trumpet to the summit of Mount Everest since that was a climb he would never make.

Kerrebrock's death shattered Wickwire. His sense of failure was profound. And his solitude—alone on the north side of North America's greatest mountain, the penetrating silence pierced only by clatter of rockfall and icefall off the Wickersham Wall—compounded his pain. Because he'd promised Kerrebrock he'd stay safe and not try to return to base camp on the Kahiltna on his own, he hunkered down beside the man-eating crevasse for five days, waiting for someone to fly over . . . and grieving.

Finally, Wickwire decided he couldn't sit idle any longer. A flyover was not guaranteed, and he needed to move, to head up toward Kahiltna Pass, where he'd have a better chance of rescue. The way was dangerous; he'd step into a series of small crevasses as he climbed, and the Wickersham Wall spit avalanches down onto his route. At the base of the pass Denali kicked up a fierce ground blizzard, which pinned him inside his bivy for four days.

Rescue came twenty days after Kerrebrock and Wickwire departed Talkeetna, when pilot Doug Geeting flew over the pass in his fixed-wing aircraft. He made a "difficult landing" on the crevassed Peters Glacier to pick up the solitary climber, then flew him back to the little town on the Susitna.

A week later, rangers and pilots from Talkeetna returned to the site of Kerrebrock's accident to recover his remains. Four men deposited by helicopter on the moraine—a ridge of rock deposited on the edge of the glacier—reported encountering more "hidden crevasses" on the Peters Glacier as they made their way to the recovery site. Mountaineering ranger Robert Gerhard rappelled into the crevasse to assess the scene while his partners rigged a Z-pulley system. Gerhard and the others spent three hours chipping away at the ice to free the dead man, who was then hoisted to the surface of the glacier and flown home.

In their analysis of the accident, Denali's mountaineering rangers determined neither Wickwire nor Kerrebrock committed a foul. Their approach had been well planned and well executed. The men were roped together, their use of a gear sled was commonplace (though such a "heavy sled may become a dangerous object" on the mountain, Gerhard noted). More to the point, Wickwire had done everything possible to save Kerrebrock's life. Wickwire's shoulder injury hampered his strength and effectiveness, and the only way the rescue party was able to free Kerrebrock was by chipping away with a small hatchet at the bulge in the crevasse wall that held him tight. Wickwire's ice ax was too big to work in the narrow slot.

"This was a freak and unusual accident and one that may be second guessed by many," Gerhard wrote in his analysis of the accident. "In my opinion, however, there is virtually nothing else Wickwire could have done to save Kerrebrock's life."

That, Jim Wickwire observed, went some way toward alleviating his feelings of guilt, of wondering if he could have done anything differently, or anything more, to save his friend and partner. That understanding, along with the gift of time and the support of his family community, enabled the mountaineer to return to the sport he loved and excelled at. He'd endure the loss of another climbing partner on Mount Everest the following year, but go on to attempt the highest summit again, as well as pioneer routes on other peaks over a long, respected career.

THE SLOT 2017

Fast forward thirty-six years. A Slovakian mountaineer named Martin Takac was on the trip of a lifetime. It was mid-June, and he was part of a guided team making its way down from the summit of Denali via the West Buttress, the most commonly used and safest route on the mountain.

Takac was partnered with a climber from the Czech Republic, both men on snowshoes. The rest of their summit team was descending on skies, and they'd already reached base camp on the Kahiltna Glacier, at about seven thousand feet. The snowshoers, not unexpectedly, had fallen behind. The weather was poor—low visibility and snow—which complicated their route finding. Takac suggested to his partner that, rather than continuing, they stop and camp—it was nearing midnight and it had been a long day. The Czech man declined and the two continued downhill, unroped, crossing a glacier upon which the snow bridges were beginning to thin.

And sure enough, one of those bridges gave way under Takac. The climber plummeted sixty feet into a crevasse that spanned about three feet at the glacier's surface, narrow enough to jump across. The thirty-eight-year-old summiter came to rest wedged between frigid walls only a foot apart, in the dark, with only a shaft of light visible above, "upstairs."

Slotted, stuck, squeezed breathless by his pack, "I was like a sandwich," Takac told Dermot Cole of *Alaska Dispatch News*.

But his rescue was underway almost immediately. Unlike Wickwire, Takac's partner was able to hail help from the nearby camp. As soon as the alarm was raised, the well-oiled Denali search-and-rescue machine kicked into high gear.

It was clear from the start that extraordinary tactics would be necessary to save the trapped man. Pulling Takac out with a rope, no matter how ingenious the pulley system, was not an option. The walls pinched

An aerial photograph taken early in the mountaineering season shows crevasses, "visible as stripes in the distance," on the Kahiltna Glacier surrounding the 7,800-foot base camp.
NATIONAL PARK SERVICE PHOTO

so tightly the first ranger lowered into the crevasse had to exhale just to descend deeper.

Time was of the essence. Not unexpectedly, Takac, who'd broken ribs in the fall and was struggling to breathe, also began to suffer from hypothermia within hours. Rescuers—a team of guides, rangers, and volunteers—cycled in and out of the fissure, first removing items from the climber's pack to give him more room to breathe, then working to widen the space between the sloping ice walls so they could pull him free. They chipped at the frozen cage by hand, with ice axes and chainsaws, with boiling water and a blowtorch.

"At one point we had a small breakthrough where we could clear one of his arms," ranger Chris Erickson told the *Anchorage Daily News*. "And at that point we clipped in his harness and we're thinking, all right! This is after 10 hours. But we start pulling and realized it was not his chest, arms or waist, it was his legs, feet and snowshoes, completely buried. They were feet lower, and every inch got tighter and tighter."

Meanwhile, Takac was fading. His experience offers some insight into Kerrebrock's last hours. The cold splintered the climber's memories of his rescue, but he recalled how difficult it was to breathe. He remembered that even while his arms were pinned, he was able to move his fingers, thinking even this small motion would help keep him from freezing. He couldn't turn his head, but he could hear the activity of his rescuers above him. He struggled to keep hopeful in the dark and cold, replaying his life "like a movie in my mind." And he despaired: "I was just waiting for when I will end, in the heaven, in the hell or maybe somebody will come for me to take me out?"

Eventually he passed out. "During the rescue," a report in the *American Alpine Journal* explains, Takac's "mental status had steadily declined, to the point where he was responsive only to pain stimuli."

A pneumatic chisel airlifted onto the glacier from Talkeetna—a tool Kerrebrock and Wickwire could have only acquired by wizardry—finally enabled rescuers to remove enough ice to free Takac. By the time the summiter was pulled to the surface, sixteen hours after he slotted in, he was "way past severe hypothermia," and suffering from kidney failure. A waiting helicopter flew him to the hospital in Fairbanks, where he spent several weeks recovering before flying home to his native Slovakia.

In their analysis of the accident, Denali's climbing rangers emphasized the risks inherent in traveling across glaciers unroped, and reflected on the tenuous nature of snow bridges, the "heuristic trap" they present to glacier travelers who might grow complacent as climber after climber crosses without incident.

The report also reaches back to Wickwire and Kerrebrock. "It is very unlikely that traditional companion-rescue techniques and tools would have extricated this climber [Takac] before he succumbed to hypothermia," the Denali rangers wrote. "A similar incident occurred in the Alaska Range in the early 1980s, involving a climbing party of two, and the patient perished at the bottom of a crevasse when the partner was unable to free his partner."

A lesson from the past informs climbers in the future. Denali's glaciers are riddled with deadly cold-storage lockers, but with hindsight and creativity, they don't have to become death traps.

AUTHOR'S NOTE: ACTS OF KINDNESS

On October 8, 2017, wildfire exploded out of Nuns Canyon in Glen Ellen, California. Wicked winds slashed the oaks, tossing limbs to the ground. I walked outside into blackness—not nighttime black, smoke black. What would become known as the Nuns Fire was devouring homes right down the hill and drawing a bead on mine. I couldn't see it, but I could smell it, feel it.

Then I saw flashing lights—the white flash of an SUV winding up the road. I rocketed toward authority, pounding barefoot down the pavement of my narrow side street. It was a bit of a miracle the driver saw me. By that point every firefighter and sheriff who knew Chauvet Road existed was battling one of the most devastating wildfires in California history. Reinforcements were pouring in from hundreds of miles away.

The driver turned toward me. He lifted his bullhorn. "You need to evacuate. You need to get out now."

Then he steered the SUV over the hill, lights flashing, bullhorn blaring. He had delivered his warning. Now he had to drive on and warn others. He had many lives to save that night, in a strange land full of red-hot embers and sideways flame. What happened to me next was up to me.

As I've researched these stories of bravery and sacrifice in Alaska, I've been struck by this truth. Search and rescue is obviously about the heroism of the firefighters or rangers or state troopers whose sole purpose in the moment is to get people out of whatever predicament they are in. But it's also about the characters they save. It's about how we interact with each other, rescuer and rescued, when uncertainty and danger invade our worlds.

The sun glints off the still waters at Hut Point in Misty Fjords National Monument.
PHOTO: TRACY SALCEDO

The other theme that sticks with me is how bottomless human kindness can be. We witnessed that kindness over and over in the days of the Wine Country fires. The collective memory of those days overflows with stories of generosity; everyone has a handful, a dozen, a hundred heartwarming tales to tell.

I can share a story from those days of uncertainty and shared loss that captures both themes and brings them home. Toward evening on that first fire day, my twenty-four-year-old son decided he needed to save our house. At that point we knew, by fluke and the bravery of a neighbor armed with a garden hose, the home had survived the initial firestorm. That didn't mean it would survive the next night.

My son drove to the barricade, was turned away, and decided to sneak into the evacuation zone on his skateboard. He made it to the property and went to work. Across the street, the jet engines that were exposed gas mains in the rubble of the neighbors' houses roared.

As darkness fell, he called and asked me to come get him. *The smoke is too thick*, he explained. *There's no power. There are no people. And I won't make it back to the car before dark on the skateboard.*

I went to get him, of course. The love in the air was thicker than the smoke.

At the barricade across the main road, the trooper absolutely refused my admittance. I tried the back way, where a second barricade blocked my passage. The second trooper asked me what I was doing.

I explained, then waited for denial; I was already pondering plan B.

"He did what?" the cop asked.

"He skateboarded to our house."

"Why would he do that?" the cop asked.

I hadn't slept for nearly forty-eight hours. I looked him in the eye and said, "Because he's an ass."

The cop looked up the empty road. He was young, earnest, respectful. I was bleary-eyed, dirty, overwhelmed, incapable of nuance. In that haggard, smoke-screened moment, we understood each other perfectly.

"Do me a favor," the cop said. "When you see him, slap him for me."

I didn't, of course. My son was a hero too. I found him in the smoldering yard, a bandanna over his mouth and nose, a bandit hauling hose.

And I was a rescuer, too, if only because I could save my boy from a miserable night in a dark, smoky, miraculous house.

This all was possible because a first responder, with a simple act of kindness, had believed in my good sense and trusted his own understanding of what we all were dealing with.

Search and rescue is as much an act of faith as it is of strength, experience, and expertise. It's about doing what should not be done, like landing aircraft on rivers and glaciers and mountaintops; like freeing a man from a crevasse with a pneumatic chisel; like pulling children from atop a car after a seismic shift sends them tumbling toward the sea. It's about pushing an old man's car out of an ice-filled ditch, leaving a cache of tinned goods and warm clothes in a remote wilderness cabin just in case. It's looking a desperate mother in the eye and letting her pass, knowing the worst is over—and that, if she and her ass of a son need it, people will be there to help.

In those crazy days when wildfire transformed my hometown, I had close encounters with rescuers that will stick with me forever. Those encounters inform every story told in this book. My hope is that readers of these stories are caught up in the drama and complication and grand scale of search and rescue, but I hope also the subtle, the gentle, and the thoughtful come through. Because when I think about rescue now, it's as much about the small moments as the big ones.

My gratitude, forever, to the rescuers.

STAY SAFE

No one wants to end a trip into the wilderness in a sled at the end of a short-haul line dangling from the belly of a helicopter. This quick and dirty list covers some of the ways you can facilitate safe travel in Alaska's backcountry—in any wild place, for that matter. It barely scratches the surface of what good instruction and experience can teach, but it outlines some simple things you can do to create a baseline of safety.

Let people know your route and when you expect to be back in contact or in the house. If you are carrying a cell phone and/or a satellite phone, explain to loved ones they won't hear from you on a regular basis—and that's OK. Chances are you won't be able to tweet your progress, and that's not the point of your adventure (hopefully). Rangers and troopers have better things to do than reassure your mother you're probably fine, just out of range.

Don't base your assumptions of risk on the adequacy of your communication devices. Remember: Calling 911 is not the answer.

Carry all the equipment you'll need to endure unplanned days and nights in the wilderness. How much you should carry will depend on where you're going and what you're doing, but you can get the beta from land managers and folks who've been there. Some basics include shelter, adequate clothing, food, first-aid equipment, a stove, and fuel for cooking and melting snow and/or purifying water. Don't rely on someone else to carry these things for you. You'll need to be self-sufficient in the event you become separated.

On any expedition, guided or with friends, solid group dynamics are key to both having a good time and the safety of any team. The classic example of how sketchy group dynamics can contribute to trouble in the wilderness is that of the 1967 Wilcox expedition on Denali, where even though other forces were at play, the breakdown of reliable working relationships between the team members played a significant role in what became a tragedy. Teammates should be prepared to follow the directions of the guide or expedition leader, but also feel free to ask questions and respectfully disagree or offer opinions. Leaders should not only lead, but also listen.

Be prepared to retreat. Former Denali mountaineering ranger Daryl Miller shared this snippet, illustrating how difficult the choice can be, but also how search and rescue thinks about it: A team attempting a traverse of the High One had already successfully ascended the West Buttress route from the Kahiltna Glacier and was working its way down the north side of the mountain. The climbers ran into trouble on the Harper Glacier; they'd already fallen into three crevasses, and they hadn't even reached the more heavily fissured Muldrow Glacier. They radioed Talkeetna in distress, but the incident commander, rather than initiating a SAR, advised the group to go back the way they'd come. They did, making their way safely off the mountain without assistance.

Know your limits, and those of your partners. What applies on any group hike or backpack also applies in Alaska's backcountry: You should only move as quickly as your slowest team member. Common sense should dictate whether you attempt to cross terrain presenting challenges—a rock wall, icefall, or swollen river—that exceed your physical capabilities or technical skills, or those of someone in your party.

Take the classes. Learn the rope work, how to rock climb, how to cross glaciers, how to read a map and compass, about wilderness first aid, and whatever else applies before venturing into Alaska's backcountry. The National Outdoor Leadership School is a good place to start; visit www .nols.edu to peruse the offerings.

Leave no trace. The beauty of open country is just that: It's open. It may be impossible to pass completely unnoticed, even in the vastness of Alaska, but whether traveling on foot, with a dogsled, or on a snow machine, mini- mize your impact. A good place to learn more about this ethic is https://lnt .org. But keep in mind that zero impact means different things in different places—such as a national park versus a national preserve—so checking in with land managers is important.

Tune in to the wild. Nature rewards caution and experience. The wind, the weather, the rivers, the ice, and the distances all have messages to convey. Use both your intuition and good sense when making decisions about whether you should continue, hunker down and wait it out, or head back the way you came.

Enjoy! Even if (or when) things get rocky, or iffy, or downright impossible, cultivate the optimism of a survivor. You may not accomplish what you expect, but you'll always come back, and you'll have a good story to tell.

ALASKA IN CONTEXT

To grasp the diversity of search and rescue in the state, a basic understanding of its geography and history is helpful. The variety of stories in this book are informed not only by the nature of the place that serves as their setting, but also by the state's complex and lively history, which has been shaped not only by the landscape but also by the people who've chosen to call it home.

GEOGRAPHIC CONTEXT

Alaska encompasses more than 660,000 square miles of tundra, taiga, coastline, glacier, mountain range, river valley, river delta, and more. The state is often broken into five geographic regions, each comprised of its own mix of topography and ecosystems. The boundaries vary from source to source, but captured in the broadest delineations, these regions include:

- Southwest, which stretches from the tip of the Aleutian Islands north to Norton Sound, and includes Kodiak Island and the delta of the Yukon River where it spills into the Bering Sea. The town of Bethel, on the mainland, is a major settlement. The Aleutian Islands are sometimes considered their own region.
- Southcentral, which stretches west from the Canadian border to the anchor of the Aleutian Peninsula, and north from the Gulf of Alaska to the arc of the Alaska Range. Anchorage is the hub of the region; it includes the Chugach mountain range, the Kenai Peninsula, and Glacier Bay.
- Southeast, the panhandle strung along the Canadian province of British Columbia. Islands supporting a thick boreal forest predominate here, as do steep peaks and volcanoes rising thousands

of feet from the sea. Juneau, the state capital, is in Southeast, as are the historic towns of Sitka, Skagway, and Ketchikan.

- Interior, the gigantic expanse of taiga and tundra at the center of the state, reaching from the Canadian border on the east toward Norton Sound on the west, and from the Alaska Range on the south to the Brooks Range in the north. The hub is Fairbanks, at the confluence of the Tanana and Chena Rivers, and the region encompasses Denali, at 20,310 feet the highest point on the North American continent.

- The Far North, which slides across the Arctic Circle and stretches over the Brooks Range to land's end on the Arctic Ocean. A single road leads from Fairbanks to Prudhoe Bay and its oil operations. Utqiaġvik, formerly Barrow, is the northernmost settlement in the state, and in the United States. Nome and Kotzebue are other notable towns, accessible only by plane, boat, or long overland traverses via dogsled or snow machine.

With a population of less than 750,000 people (about half of those residing in Anchorage), swaths of wilderness the size of entire states in the Lower 48 are devoid of anyone who might need, or provide, search and rescue. But the population centers in each region are primed to look out for their own, as are those living in the remotest bush villages. The ability to conduct any search and rescue, as mentioned in the introduction, is informed by those who know the terrain best.

HISTORICAL CONTEXT

To understand the cultural foundation of Alaska's search-and-rescue ethos, it's helpful to reflect on how the Last Frontier was settled. You'd think this forbidding land would have been just a stopover in prehistoric times, that people crossing the Bering land bridge fourteen thousand years ago would have just kept moving south to warmer climes. In the Far North the sun doesn't rise for months in wintertime, and doesn't set for months in summer. Though not as daunting as winter temperatures, the midnight sun presents its own exhausting challenges.

But the ancestors of today's Athabascans, Iñupiats, Gwich'in, Yupiks, Tlingits, Haida, Aleuts, and others settled and prospered on the tundra, along the coastlines, and in the forests. Their populations and enduring, enviable cultures were sustained by rich food sources on land and sea, with salmon, caribou, whale, and fruits on the menu. Those same animals, as well as trees and shrubs, provided supplies for clothing, housing, and means of transportation for a seasonally nomadic lifestyle on land as well as for seafaring.

European colonization began in 1741, when Russian explorers ventured beyond the boundaries of Siberia, their own Far North. Vitas Bering was among the first to arrive; he was followed by others seeking wealth through the fur trade. The Russian legacy is still evident in towns along the coastline from Kodiak to the islands of the Inside Passage, where New Archangel, now Sitka, served as colonial capital.

The Russians had a profound and destructive impact on Alaska's First Peoples, spreading disease, upending economies, disrupting cultures, and generally wreaking imperial havoc. But the American northlands ultimately proved too remote and inhospitable for serious Russian expansion. When William Seward, then secretary of state for President Andrew Jackson, offered to purchase the vast territory for $7.2 million—or about two cents per acre, ridiculously cheap by today's standards but considered a folly in Seward's day—the czar agreed. Alaska became an American territory in 1867, and remained so until it became the forty-ninth state in 1959.

Throughout the 1800s and into the early 1900s, polar exploration was all the global rage. The Northwest Passage was both a promise and a mystery, sparking legendary explorations into the Arctic; the antipode, the Antarctic, inspired similar adventures. In those years, Alaska search and rescue meshed sea with land: When the oceans froze, ships became icebound—essentially landlocked—and rescue missions like the one John Muir joined in 1881 were launched.

In 1896 gold was discovered in the Klondike River, and a rush to Canada's Yukon Territory ensued. Once again the lives of Alaska's native peoples were transformed, as were the lives of the scattered white immigrants who settled the territory. Prospectors flooded north to "moil for gold," and those who didn't die or head back home when the boom went bust followed the color down the Yukon River and into Alaska. New goldfields were discovered (and quickly depleted) in Fairbanks, then Nome, and in small towns along other tributaries throughout the wilderness. Though the living was hardscrabble, the Klondike rush resulted in a population explosion, with thousands of starry-eyed and hopelessly unprepared men and women pouring through mountain passes and down flooding rivers. In those days Alaskan search and rescue assumed a land-bound aspect, but went mostly unheralded. For every story of a miner saving a freezing fellow miner from certain death by dragging him into a shack where a fire warmed the frigid air, likely a hundred have gone untold. But on at least one occasion miners rose to an extraordinary challenge, using their picks and shovels to dig a host of their comrades out of avalanche debris that swept across the long, treacherous, Chilkoot Trail.

Alaska's strategic location on the world stage took on renewed significance in World War II. In June 1942 Japan seized two islands, Kiska and Attu, in the Aleutians, justifying a military buildup that remains integral to American security into modern times. Spurred by the Japanese invasion and other wartime interests, an influx of troops and munitions flowed northward from the Lower 48 along a road men cut as they went—the Alaska Highway, or Alcan, built over the course of a year and spanning about seventeen hundred miles from Dawson Creek in British Columbia to Fairbanks.

During the war, Ladd Army Airfield in Fairbanks became central to the Lend-Lease program, through which America was able to move equipment and supplies to its Allies, including the Soviet Union. Bush pilots had already established the importance of air travel in the territory, but the war effort solidified and expanded its influence. Aviation became a staple of Alaskan transportation—now distant villages in the Interior and on remote reaches of coastline could be accessed by something faster and more modern than dogsled. Military resources and expertise could be incorporated into search-and-rescue efforts if needed. On the flip side, pilots exploring what was possible for man and machine in extreme cold, wind, and storm—such as the amazing Leon Crane and his crewmates—could find they'd pushed past the limits and were in dire straits. Sometimes rescue was possible; sometimes man and machine were lost.

The landscape for search and rescue changed again in 1980 when, after years of contentious negotiation, Congress passed the Alaska National Interest Lands Conservation Act (ANILCA). Signed into law by President Jimmy Carter, this complicated and controversial legislation redefined the boundaries of the state's public lands and how those lands could be used, reconfiguring rules governing access, jurisdiction, and hunting, trapping, and subsistence gathering. With ANILCA, more than a hundred million acres of wilderness became a national commons, conserved as new and expanded national parks and preserves, monuments, wildlife refuges, and more. This massive expansion of the public land trust drew a fresh batch of explorers and adventurers to newly protected federal wildernesses with glorious names like Gates of the Arctic, Wrangell-St. Elias, Kobuk Valley, and Katmai. ANILCA also moved National Park Service rangers, and in particular the rangers of Denali National Park and Preserve, to the forefront of search and rescue on those lands.

Today, tourism is a major economic driver in Alaska. The national parks and preserves are among the state's most attractive destinations. Nearly three million people ventured to Alaskan national parks in 2018, spending more than $1.3 billion and generating nearly eighteen thousand jobs. Klondike Gold Rush National Historical Park, Denali National Park and Preserve, and Glacier Bay National Park and Preserve were the most popular destinations. Denali outpaces the rest when it comes to search and rescue—no surprise, given the lure of climbing (or simply seeing) one of the most impressive peaks on the planet. But as more people venture into remote wilderness-become-parkland, into places once known only to caribou and wolves, the odds increase that search-and-rescue operations in those faraway places will become more frequent.

DEDICATION AND ACKNOWLEDGMENTS

As always, my thanks and love to my sons, Jesse, Cruz, and Penn, who grow more dear as they fly farther from home, and who persist in making sure, no matter what the job, I keep it real. You are my homegrown adventure and my enduring heroes. This book is dedicated to you.

This book would not have been possible without the gifts of time and storytelling from Daryl Miller, Roger Robinson, and Mark Westman, rangers and mountaineers with Denali National Park and Preserve. I also owe debts of gratitude to Denali's public information officer Maureen Gualtieri, museum curator Kim Arthur, and park historian Erik Johnson, and to other park service sources, including Eric Bensen, Lindy Mihata, and Rebecca Talbott at the National Park Service's Alaska Regional Office.

I picked the brains of a number of folks to gather insights on Alaskan search and rescue, both in person and on the telephone, in Talkeetna, Anchorage (thank you, Pat Rastall), Sitka, and beyond. Vern Tejas did me the favor of telling me his story and reviewing my retelling. I don't know the names of all the friendly strangers in coffee shops and living rooms and roadhouses along the lovely, lonely road linking Anchorage to Fairbanks who shared stories or observations with me, but I am grateful.

A number of writers and friends closer to home have provided support and encouragement as I've composed these stories. They include Arthur and Jill Dawson, Ann and Alec Peters, Ed Davis, Fran Meininger, and Jim Shere. Editor and friend Patrice Fusillo always has my back. Folks a bit farther afield who inform my work include Kelly Knappe, Karen Charland, Julianne Roth, my parents, Jesse and Judy Salcedo, and the Chourré, Friedman, and Rodman clans.

Editor Holly Rubino was a patient guide through the long, often interrupted process of pulling this book together. I am grateful for her patience and guidance. Thanks also to Kristen Mellitt for ushering the book through the production process and for her patience as well.

Thanks again and always to Sara Bergendahl, my kindred spirit and sister across several decades and thousands of miles. She knows one year I'll find my way to Sitka in the dead of winter and fall in love again, as I have in spring, summer, and autumn. She suspects (as do I) that Alaska is home, and that I've just not found the way yet.

BIBLIOGRAPHY AND SELECTED SOURCES

Significant sources for several rescue stories on Denali included correspondence and reports contained in the archives housed in the Denali National Park and Preserve museum. Specific reports are listed below in Selected Sources and Sites.

Project Jukebox, part of the University of Alaska-Fairbanks's Oral History Program, produced a series of recordings and other media chronicling mountaineering on Denali, as well as other notable Alaskan climbers, pilots, and adventurers. To hear interviews with Jim Wickwire, Art Davidson, Cliff Hudson, Daryl Miller, Roger Robinson, Brad Washburn, and more, visit https://jukebox.uaf.edu/site7/denali.

Another amazing resource for those interested in search and rescue as well as survival is the *Sharp End*, a podcast produced by the American Alpine Club from *Accidents in North American Climbing*. To listen to the podcast interview with Malcolm Daly, or any of the other fascinating stories compiled by the organization, visit https://americanalpineclub.org/sharp-end-podcast.

The websites of every national park in America are reservoirs of fascinating stories and authenticated information. The list below includes some of the articles I referenced for research purposes. Click on the embedded links on any of the Alaska National Park sites and you'll open a wealth of additional information, with more embedded links to explore. I expect you, like me, will be enthralled by the well-researched and engagingly presented stories in these curated rabbit holes.

I spent hours in Denali National Park and Preserve's Walter Harper Ranger Station in Talkeetna studying articles in the collection of *American Alpine Journals* stashed in the conference room. The *AAJ* also has compiled its compilations of accident reports online at http://publications.american alpineclub.org. These proved an invaluable source for understanding and chronicling search-and-rescue operations throughout Alaska.

BOOKS

Berton, Pierre. *The Klondike Fever: The Life and Death of the Last Great Gold Rush*. New York: Carroll & Graf, 1970.

Browne, Belmore. *The Conquest of Mount McKinley*. New York: G. P. Putnam's Sons, 1913.

Cook, Frederick Albert. *To the Top of the Continent*. London: Hodder & Stoughton, 1909.

Davidson, Art. *Minus 148°: The First Winter Ascent of Mount McKinley*. Rev. ed. Seattle, WA: Mountaineers Books, 2013.

Drury, Bob. *The Rescue Season: The Heroic Story of the Parajumpers on the Edge of the World*. New York: Simon & Schuster, 2001.

Dunn, Robert. *The Shameless Diary of an Explorer*. Rev. ed. Big Byte Books, 2010. First published 1907 by Outing Publishing (New York).

Fountain, Henry. *The Great Quake: How the Biggest Earthquake in North America Changed Our Understanding of the Planet*. New York: Crown, 2017.

Gonzales, Laurence. *Deep Survival: Who Lives, Who Dies, and Why*. New York: W. W. Norton, 2017.

Greiner, James. *Wager with the Wind: The Don Sheldon Story*. New York: St. Martin's Press, 1974.

Hall, Andy. *Denali's Howl: The Deadliest Climbing Disaster on America's Wildest Peak*. New York: Dutton, 2014.

Heacox, Kim. *Rhythm of the Wild: A Life Inspired by Alaska's Denali National Park*. Guilford, CT: Lyons Press, 2015.

Jans, Nick. *The Grizzly Maze: Timothy Treadwell's Fatal Obsession with Alaskan Bears*. East Rutherford, NJ: Penguin, 2006.

Miller, Debbie. *The Great Serum Race: Blazing the Iditarod Trail*. New York: Walker & Co., 2002.

Muir, John. *The Cruise of the Corwin.* Sierra Club, 1917. https://vault
.sierraclub.org/john_muir_exhibit/writings/cruise_of_the_corwin/.

Muir, John. *Travels in Alaska.* New York: Firework Press. First published
1914.

Murphy, Brian. *81 Days below Zero: The Incredible Survival Story of a World
War II Pilot in Alaska's Frozen Wilderness.* Boston, MA: Da Capo Press,
2015.

9.2: Kodiak and the World's Second Largest Earthquake. Kodiak, AK: *Kodiak
Daily Mirror* and the Baranov Museum, 2013.

Norris, Frank. *The Crown Jewel of the North: An Administrative History of
Denali National Park and Preserve,* vols. 1 and 2. Alaska Regional Office
of the National Park Service, Anchorage, Alaska, 2006.

Pearson, Grant, and Philip Newill. *My Life of High Adventure.* Englewood
Cliffs, NJ: Prentice-Hall, 1962. Available online at archive.org/details/
mylifeofhighadve012794mbp.

Salcedo, Tracy. *Historic Denali National Park and Preserve: The Stories
behind One of America's Great Treasures.* Guilford, CT: Lyons Press,
2017.

Salisbury, Gay, and Laney Salisbury. *The Cruelest Miles: The Heroic Story of
Dogs and Men in a Race against an Epidemic.* New York: W. W. Norton,
2005.

Sandler, Martin. *The Impossible Rescue: The True Story of an Amazing Arctic
Adventure.* Somerville, MA: Candlewick Press, 2012.

Service, Robert. *The Best of Robert Service.* Toronto: McGraw-Hill Ryerson,
1940.

Settle, Jimmy, and Don Reardon. *Never Quit.* New York: St. Martin's
Press, 2017.

Sides, Hampton. *In the Kingdom of Ice: The Grand and Terrible Polar Voyage
of the USS Jeannette.* New York: Random House, 2014.

Stuck, Hudson. *The Ascent of Denali.* New York: Charles Scribner's Sons,
1918.

Tejas, Vern, and Lew Freedman. *Seventy Summits: Life in the Mountains.*
Indianapolis, IN: Blue River Press, 2017.

United States Revenue Cutter Service. *Report of the Cruise of the U. S. Revenue Cutter Bear and the Overland Expedition for the Relief of the Whalers in the Arctic Ocean from November 27, 1897, to September 13, 1898.* U.S. Government Printing Office, 1899.

Walker, Tom. *Kantishna: Mushers, Miners, Mountaineers: The Pioneer Story behind Mount McKinley National Park.* Missoula, MT: Pictorial Histories, 2005.

———. *The Seventymile Kid: The Lost Legacy of Harry Karstens and the First Ascent of Mount McKinley.* Seattle, WA: Mountaineers Books, 2013.

Ward, Kennan. *Denali: Reflections of a Naturalist.* Minnetonka, MN: NorthWood Press, 2000.

Waterman, Jonathan. *Chasing Denali: The Sourdoughs, Cheechakos, and Frauds behind the Most Unbelievable Feat in Mountaineering.* Guilford, CT: Lyons Press, 2018.

———. *In the Shadow of Denali: Life and Death on Alaska's Mt. McKinley.* New York: Random House, 1994.

———. *Surviving Denali: A Study of Accidents on Mount McKinley 1903–1990.* Golden, CO: American Alpine Club Press, 1982.

Where Were You? Alaska Earthquake 1964. Compilation by various authors. Homer Public Library, Homer, Alaska, 1996.

Whittaker, Lou, and Andrea Gabbard. *Lou Whittaker: Memoirs of a Mountain Guide.* Seattle, WA: Mountaineers Books, 1994.

Wickersham, James, and Terrence Cole. *Old Yukon: Tales, Trails, and Trials.* Reprint. Anchorage, AK: University of Alaska Press, 2010.

SELECTED SOURCES AND SITES

The Aerial Perspective. Aircraft in Denali National Park: Where Did It Start? https://tgeorgeonline.wordpress.com/2009/04/09/aircraft-in-denali-national-park-where-did-it-start/

Air Mobility Command Museum. Operation Helping Hand. https://amc museum.org/history/operation-helping-hand/

American Alpine Journal. Crevasse Fall and 15-Hour Rescue: Climbing Unroped. 2018. http://publications.americanalpineclub.org/

articles/13201214808/Crevasse-Fall-and-15-Hour-Rescue-Climbing
-Unroped
——. Falling Ice, Fall on Ice, Ice Screw Failed. 2000. http://publications
.americanalpineclub.org/articles/13200002200/Falling-Ice-Fall-on-Ice
-Ice-Screw-Failed
——. Fall into Crevasse, Alaska, Mount McKinley. 1982.
http://publications.americanalpineclub.org/articles/13198202200/
Fall-into-Crevasse-Alaska-Mount-McKinley
——. Fall on Snow: Failure to Clip in to Fixed Rope. 2012. http://
publications.americanalpineclub.org/articles/13201201700/
Fall-on-Snow-Failure-to-Clip-in-to-Fixed-Rope
——. Overdue Climbers: Disappeared, Probably Perished in a Snow Cave
from Hypothermia and/or Asphyxiation, Lost Pack Containing Crit-
ically Needed Supplies, Weather. 2007. http://publications.american
alpineclub.org/articles/13200700902/Overdue-ClimbersDisappeared
-Probably-Perished-in-a-Snow-Cave-from-Hypothermia-andor
-Asphyxiation-Lost-Pack-Containing-Critically-Needed-Supplies
-Weather
——. Serac Fall, Alaska, Mount Johnson, Ruth Gorge. 2001. http://
publications.americanalpineclub.org/articles/13200102200/
Serac-Fall-Alaska-Mount-Johnson-Ruth-Gorge
Anchorage Daily News. Searchers Find Snowmachine Belonging to Man
Missing on Norton Bay. April 4, 2016. https://www.adn.com/rural
-alaska/article/searchers-find-snowmobile-belonging-missing-man
-anchorage-alaska-ap-searchers-using/2016/04/04/
Anchorage Daily Times. Helga Bading Hasn't Lost Desire To Reach Top Of
Mt. McKinley. May 23, 1960.
Associated Press. Boy, 9, Disappears into Glacier Crevasse on
Snowmobile. April 15, 2013. https://www.thestar.com/news/
world/2013/04/15/boy_9_disappears_into_glacier_crevasse_on_
snowmobile.html
——. Community Grieves over Plane Crash. *Los Angeles Times*, June 22,
2000. http://articles.latimes.com/2000/jun/22/news/mn-43784

———. Polish Climber Told: Can't Return to U.S. *Daily Sitka Sentinel,* September 15, 1992. https://www.newspapers.com/image/22174893/?terms=Wiecha

Berg, Glen V., and James L. Stratta. Anchorage and the Alaska Earthquake of March 27, 1964. American Iron and Steel Institute, New York, NY, 1964.

Berliner, Jeff. Polish Climber Hospitalized after McKinley Ordeal. UPI, July 8, 1991. https://www.upi.com/Archives/1991/07/08/Polish-climber-hospitalized-after-McKinley-ordeal/7548678945600/

Berry, Lt. J. G. Reindeer Are Driven into Point Barrow. *San Francisco Call,* July 18, 1898. https://www.newspapers.com/image/81004651/?terms=Jarvis

Bowers, Don. History of Iditarod: The Last Great Race. 2012. https://iditarod.com/about/history/

Canadian Press. Flyer Lost 84 Days in Frigid Wilds of Yukon. *Philadelphia Inquirer,* March 17, 1944. https://www.newspapers.com/image/171526377

———. Victim Tells of Plane's Fate after 84 Days in North's Wilds. https://www.newspapers.com/image/414062642/?terms=Leon%2BCrane

Cape Girardeau Democrat. Affairs at Sheep Camp. April 23, 1898. https://www.newspapers.com/image/148693556/?terms=chilkoot%2Btrail%2Bavalanche

CBS News. Avalanche Rescuers Losing Hope. May 22, 1999. https://www.cbsnews.com/news/avalanche-rescuers-losing-hope/

Chugach National Forest Avalanche Information Center. http://www.cnfaic.org/accidents/accidents.php

Cole, Dermot. Thirty-five Years Ago, Carter Drew Wrath of Many Alaskans. *Anchorage Daily News,* November 13, 2013. https://www.adn.com/commentary/article/thirty-five-years-ago-carter-drew-wrath-many-alaskans/2013/12/01/

Crane, Leon. I Was Lost 84 Days in the Arctic. *American Magazine,* 1944.

Csizmazia, Kim. Gone. *Alpinist* (blog), June 1, 2007. http://www.alpinist.com/doc/ALP20/features-gone-csizmazia

Denali National Park and Preserve Annual Mountaineering Summaries. https://www.nps.gov/dena/planyourvisit/mountaineering-summary-reports.htm

Dunham, Mike. Seismic Shift: How the 1964 Alaska Earthquake Changed Science. *Anchorage Daily News*, March 23, 2014. https://www.adn.com/alaska-news/article/seismic-shift-how-1964-alaska-earthquake-changed-science/2014/03/24/

———. Survivor to Recall Deadly '54 Denali Climb. *Anchorage Daily News*, June 25, 2011. https://www.adn.com/alaska-news/article/survivor-recall-deadly-54-denali-climb/2011/06/26/

Eckel, Edwin B. The Alaska Earthquake March 27, 1964: Lessons and Conclusions. US Geological Survey, 1970. http://dggs.alaska.gov/web pubs/usgs/p/text/p0546.pdf

Fesler, Don, and Jill Fredston. Turnagain Pass Avalanche Accident Report, March 21, 1999. Avalanche Mountain Safety Center, May 5, 1999. http://www.cnfaic.org/accidents/1999_RepeatOffender_PublicVersion.pdf

Glasgow Herald. The Klondike Disaster. April 29, 1898. https://www.newspapers.com/image/409208613/?terms=chilk oot%2Btrail%2Bavalanche

Gross, Scott. "Mushin' Mortician" Honored for Iditarod Rescue. KTVA, July 12, 2018. https://www.ktva.com/story/38633197/mushin-mortician-honored-for-iditarod-rescue

Hanlon, Tegan. "Truly a Legend": Champion of First Iditarod Dies at 75. *Anchorage Daily News*, March 28, 2018;. https://www.adn.com/outdoors-adventure/iditarod/2018/03/28/truly-a-legend-champion-of-the-first-iditarod-dies-at-age-75/

Iditarod 46 (blog). Iditarod Unveils 2018 Purse Spread. March 21, 2018. http://www.ktva.com/story/37596792/iditarod-46-live-race-blog

James, David. Mail Carriers a Vital Part of Alaska's History. *Fairbanks Daily News-Miner*, May 19, 2012. http://www.newsminer.com/sports/yukon_quest/mail-carriers-a-vital-part-of-alaska-s-history/article_ad152f05-ee09-565d-9208-8a14e46be5df.html

Jenkins, Mark. Infinite Sorrow: The Disappearance of Two of North America's Best Alpinists Left a Grave Question: What Happens When the Only Way Out Is Up? Outside Online, August 24, 2006. https://www.outsideonline.com/1909631/infinite-sorrow

Johnson, Crane, and Rick Thoman. Alaska River Breakup: Historic Comparison and 2017 Spring Outlook. National Weather Service, April 11, 2017. https://accap.uaf.edu/sites/default/files/Brkup17_ACCAP_bcj_thoman_compressed.pdf

Johnston, John. Report of Rescue Operations on Mount McKinley, Alaska, May 17–26, 1960.

Kid's Health. Diphtheria. https://kidshealth.org/en/parents/diphtheria.html

Lynn, Capi. A Mountain of Memories and the Loss of a Husband. *Statesman-Journal* (Salem, Oregon), July 9, 2004. https://www.newspapers.com/image/202258415/?terms=Berniece%2BThayer

MacDonald, Dougald. Remembering Denali's Greatest Rescue. *Climbing*, June 15, 2012. https://www.climbing.com/people/band-of-brothers-andndash-remembering-denalis-greatest-rescue/

Mayo Clinic. Diphtheria. https://www.mayoclinic.org/diseases-conditions/diphtheria/symptoms-causes/syc-20351897

McGee, Madeline. I've Lived in Anchorage for Four Weeks: Here's What the Earthquake Taught Me about Alaskans. *Anchorage Daily News*, December 8, 2018. https://www.adn.com/opinions/2018/12/09/ive-lived-in-anchorage-for-four-weeks-heres-what-the-earthquake-taught-me-about-alaskans/

Medred, Craig. An Alaska Life Lived Large. *Anchorage Daily News*, February 7, 2009. https://www.adn.com/alaska-news/article/alaska-life-lived-large/2009/02/08/

———. Unexpected Rescue (blog post). April 18, 2018. https://craigmedred.news/2018/04/18/unexpected-rescue/

Mondor, Colleen. Search and Rescue Flights on Denali Gave Don Sheldon Place in Alaska Lore. *Anchorage Daily News*, June 22, 2013. https://www.adn.com/bush-pilot/article/search-and-rescue-flights-denali-gave-don-sheldon-place-alaska-lore/2013/06/23/

Mountain Zone. Triumph and Tragedy: The Mountain Zone Interviews: Jim Wickwire. https://www.mountainzone.com/climbing/misc/wickwire/

National Aeronautics and Space Administration. Cosmic Rays. https://imagine.gsfc.nasa.gov/science/toolbox/cosmic_rays1.html

National Oceanic and Atmospheric Administration. Turnagain Heights Landslide, Anchorage, Alaska. https://www.ngdc.noaa.gov/hazardimages/picture/show/151

National Park Service. An Introduction to Short-Haul Operations. Super Huge Films. https://vimeo.com/111570727

———. A WWII Survival Story from the Charley River. Yukon-Charley Rivers National Preserve. https://www.nps.gov/yuch/learn/history-culture/leon-crane-survival-story.htm

———. National Park Tourism in Alaska Creates $1.3 Billion in Economic Benefit. April 20, 2017. https://www.nps.gov/kefj/learn/news/national-park-tourism-in-alaska-creates-economic-benefit.htm

———. The Lend-Lease Program and the Alaska-Siberia Route. https://www.nps.gov/Nr/twhp/wwwlps/lessons/146LaddField/146facts2.htm

———. The Palm Sunday Avalanche. Klondike Gold Rush National Historical Park. https://www.nps.gov/articles/palm-sunday-avalanche.htm

———. The Russians. Sitka National Historical Park. https://www.nps.gov/sitk/learn/historyculture/the-russians.htm

———. Tourism in Alaska's National Parks Creates $1.3 Billion in Economic Benefit. April 26, 2018. https://www.nps.gov/orgs/1840/tourism-benefits-2017-update.htm

Naval History and Heritage Command. The Incredible Alaska Overland Rescue. https://www.history.navy.mil/content/history/nhhc/research/library/online-reading-room/title-list-alphabetically/i/incredible-alaska-overland-rescue.html

Newsweek. Deathwatch on Mount Mckinley. June 7, 1992. https://www.newsweek.com/deathwatch-mount-mckinley-199464

Nome Convention and Visitors Bureau. A Race for Life: Balto and the Hero Dogs of Alaska. http://www.visitnomealaska.com/wp-content/

uploads/2015/04/A-Race-for-Life-Balto-and-the-Hero-Dogs-of
-Alaska.pdf

——. The 1925 Serum Run to Nome. https://www.visitnomealaska
.com/wp-content/uploads/2015/04/The-1925-Serum-Run-to-Nome
.pdf

Olson, Dean F. Alaska Reindeer Herdsmen: A Study of Native Manage-
ment in Transition. Institute of Social, Economic and Government
Research, University of Alaska, Fairbanks, 1969. http://www.alaskool
.org/projects/reindeer/history/iser1969/rdeer_1.html

O'Malley, Julia. March 27, 1964: The Day the Earth Fell to Pieces for One
Anchorage Family. *Anchorage Daily News*, March 22, 2014. https://
www.adn.com/our-alaska/article/march-27-1964-day-earth-fell
-pieces-one-anchorage-family/2014/03/23/

Oskin, Becky. Facts about the 1964 Alaska Earthquake. Live Science,
March 27, 2014. https://www.livescience.com/44412-1964-alaska
-earthquake-facts.html

Pearson, Grant. Climbing Down McKinley. *The Alaska Sportsman*, January
1945.

Pratt, Rupert. Survivor of 1954 C-47 Crash Thinks "Scale Needs Bal-
ancing." *Mat-Su Valley Frontiersman*, October 20, 2004. https://www
.frontiersman.com/opinion/survivor-of-c--crash-thinks-scale-needs
-balancing/article_c6890970-93e9-506c-9ddb-3de3f7d008ba.html

Quinn, Paul. Bad Weather Delays Removal of 30–40 McKinley Climbers.
UPI/*Anchorage Daily News*, May 23, 1960.

Rosen, Yereth. In Aftermath of Giant Quake, Anchorage Allowed
Rebuilding in Slide-Prone Turnagain Area. *Anchorage Daily News*,
March 24, 2014. https://www.adn.com/alaska-news/article/aftermath
-giant-quake-anchorage-allowed-rebuilding-slide-prone-turnagain
-area/2014/03/25/

Samuel, Ben. A Jewish Flyer Thru Coldest Alaska. *Wisconsin Jewish Chron-
icle*, July 21, 1944. https://www.newspapers.com/image/49958864/
?terms=Leon%2BCrane

Saul, Joshua. The Last Brother. *Anchorage Daily News*, April 15, 2010.
https://www.adn.com/alaska-news/article/last-brother/2010/04/16/

Sherbs, Diana. The Long Blue Line: Lt. David Jarvis. *Coast Guard Compass*, October 22, 2015. http://coastguard.dodlive.mil/2015/10/the-long-blue-line-lt-david-jarvis/

Slomski, Anita, and Douglas Beckstead. The Long Trip Home. *Parks*, Fall 2007. http://www.emblemaviation.com/wp-content/uploads/2012/06/The-Long-Trip-Home.pdf

Smithsonian. The Great Nome Gold Rush. National Postal Museum. https://postalmuseum.si.edu/gold/nome.html

Snyder, Jodi. Hudson Air Service: A Big Part of Talkeetna History. *Frontiersman*, July 13, 2004. https://www.frontiersman.com/valley_life/hudson-air-service-a-big-part-of-talkeetna-history/article_82fe9433-ca29-5746-a1eb-5535cb88281d.html

Strobridge, Thomas. Operation Helping Hand: The US Army and the Alaskan Earthquake, 27 March to 7 May, 1964. US Army historian in Anchorage.

Sturm, Matthew. Climbing into Catastrophe. *Heartland*, June 9, 2000, Fairbanks, Alaska.

Taylor, Alan. 1964: Alaska's Good Friday Earthquake. *The Atlantic*, May 30, 2014. https://www.theatlantic.com/photo/2014/05/1964-alaskas-good-friday-earthquake/100746/

Thompson, John. "I'm Not Going to Make It": Janssen Describes Iditarod Rescue. KTVA, March 16, 2018. http://www.ktva.com/story/37746650/im-not-going-to-make-it-janssen-describes-iditarod-rescue

Tizon, Alex. In the Land of Missing Persons. *The Atlantic*, April 2016. https://www.theatlantic.com/magazine/archive/2016/04/in-the-land-of-missing-persons/471477/

Tizon, Tomas Alex. Alaska, Land of the Lost. *Los Angeles Times*, February 5, 2005. http://articles.latimes.com/2005/feb/15/nation/na-vanished15

US Department of Defense. Airman Missing from WWII Is Identified. *Arlington National Cemetery*, 2007. http://www.arlingtoncemetery.net/hehoskin.htm

US Geological Survey. Earthquake Hazards Program. 1964 Alaska Earthquake Damage Photos. https://earthquake.usgs.gov/earthquakes/events/alaska1964/1964pics.php

———. Largest Earthquake in Alaska. 1993. https://earthquake.usgs.gov/earthquakes/events/alaska1964/largest_in_alaska.php

White, Rindi. Bush Pilot Hudson Inexorably Linked to Mountain, Climbers. *Anchorage Daily News*, March 9, 2010. https://www.adn.com/alaska-news/article/bush-pilot-hudson-inexorably-linked-mountain-climbers/2010/03/10/

Wood, Morton S. The First Traverse of Mt. McKinley: A First Ascent of the South Buttress. *American Alpine Club*, 1954. http://publications.americanalpineclub.org/articles/12195505100/The-First-Traverse-of-Mt-McKinley-A-First-Ascent-of-the-South-Buttress

ABOUT THE AUTHOR

Tracy Salcedo is the author of *Historic Yosemite National Park*, *Historic Denali National Park and Preserve*, and *Death in Mount Rainier National Park*. She's also written FalconGuides to a number of destinations, including *Hiking Northern California Waterfalls*, *Hiking through History San Francisco*, *Best Hikes Reno and Lake Tahoe*, and *Hiking Lassen Volcanic National Park*. Her titles in the Best Easy Day Hikes series include San Francisco's Peninsula, North Bay, and East Bay, as well as Lake Tahoe, San Jose, Reno, Sacramento, Boulder, Denver, and Aspen. When not writing, she works as an editor and librarian. She lives with her family in California's Wine Country. You can learn more by visiting her website at www.laughingwaterink.com.